THE TEN COMMANDMENTS
OF LEAN SIX SIGMA

PRAISE FOR *THE TEN COMMANDMENTS OF LEAN SIX SIGMA*:

I am delighted to finally see a well-structured Lean Six Sigma book that focuses on the behavioural and cultural necessities for successful Lean Six Sigma programs rather than on the use of tools and techniques. The authors have drawn upon their vast experiences working with Operational Excellence programs across diverse industries to bring us the absolute must-have components for success.

— **John Dennis**, Chairman, International Lean Six Sigma Institute, UK

I would recommend this book as it captures the essence of results-based references to the tools and concepts required in a structured way to achieve the process of implementing the leverage of Lean Six Sigma to maximise efficiencies and maintain the managerial process. Every business needs to revisit and discover how to propel your organisation to new levels of competitive success this book will support and guide you.

— **Michael Mitchell**, Managing Director, Bespoke Clinical Care Ltd, UK

The Ten Commandments of Lean Six Sigma *brings together the leading authors of our time and presents a unique guide for any leadership team as they embark on their LSS journey. The final chapter on the future of LSS is a must read for established LSS practitioners.*

— **Stephen G Anthony**, Master Black Belt and CEO of the Institute of Six Sigma Professionals, Wales, UK

In today's competitive world, any firm needs to be conscious of quality, cost and timely delivery. To achieve this, the book The Ten Commandments of Lean Six Sigma *will be a very useful guide for practitioners. The book addresses all that is required by the*

practitioners to implement LSS in their respective organizations. This book aims to transfer the knowledge that is available with the academic world for its practical application in the competitive business world.

— *S Navaneetha Krishnan*, Senior Deputy General Manager at Warship Design Centre, Larsen & Toubro and Commander (Retd), Indian Navy

The authors' experience with training in both academic and industrial settings are evident, as the methods prescribed for preparing individuals for LSS execution are applicable to both scenarios and will likewise prepare the reader for either. They understand that it is not enough to be technically proficient, in order to be a successful LSS practitioner, and they offer solid advice in the critically required soft skills, as well. This book will help any organization preparing to embark upon the continuous improvement journey.

— *David W. Hoffa*, PhD, ASQ CSSBB, External Process Engineering Manager, Johnson & Johnson

This book is definitely a new piece of art in Lean Six Sigma literature! The authors present an exceptional combination of rigorous literature review and solid pragmatic recommendations addressing critical topics in Lean Six Sigma from top to bottom. Content is brilliantly presented in an understandable language and the sequencing of commandments flows smoothly and logically in a way that you just can't stop reading.

— *Marcelo Machado Fernandes*, PhD, ASQ Certified Master Black Belt, Lean Six Sigma Consultant at FCV and SETA, Consultant at Minitab LLC, Founder of MF Treinamentos (MF Operational Excellence), Brazil

THE TEN COMMANDMENTS OF LEAN SIX SIGMA

A Guide for Practitioners

JIJU ANTONY
Heriot Watt University, UK

VIJAYA SUNDER M.
The World Bank Group, India

CHAD LAUX
Purdue University, USA

ELIZABETH CUDNEY
Missouri University of Science and Technology, USA

United Kingdom – North America – Japan
India – Malaysia – China

Emerald Publishing Limited
Howard House, Wagon Lane, Bingley BD16 1WA, UK

First edition 2020

Copyright © 2020 Emerald Publishing Limited

Reprints and permissions service
Contact: permissions@emeraldinsight.com

No part of this book may be reproduced, stored in a retrieval system, transmitted in any form or by any means electronic, mechanical, photocopying, recording or otherwise without either the prior written permission of the publisher or a licence permitting restricted copying issued in the UK by The Copyright Licensing Agency and in the USA by The Copyright Clearance Center. Any opinions expressed in the chapters are those of the authors. Whilst Emerald makes every effort to ensure the quality and accuracy of its content, Emerald makes no representation implied or otherwise, as to the chapters' suitability and application and disclaims any warranties, express or implied, to their use.

British Library Cataloguing in Publication Data
A catalogue record for this book is available from the British Library

ISBN: 978-1-78973-690-8 (Print)
ISBN: 978-1-78973-687-8 (Online)
ISBN: 978-1-78973-689-2 (Epub)

INVESTOR IN PEOPLE

Dedicated to our parents and families

TABLE OF CONTENTS

List of Figures	*xiii*
List of Tables	*xv*
About the Authors	*xvii*
Preface	*xxi*
Acknowledgements	*xxiii*

1. Introduction to Lean Six Sigma and Ten Commandments — 1
   1.1 Introduction to Lean and Six Sigma — 1
   1.2 Why Is the Integration of Lean and Six Sigma a Better Approach for Problem-solving? — 3
   1.3 LSS Methodology: An Overview — 5
   1.4 An Overview of the Ten Commandments of LSS — 6
   1.5 Summary — 8

2. Alignment of Lean Six Sigma with Organisational Strategy — 9
   2.1 Introduction — 9
   2.2 Need for Aligning LSS with Organisational Strategy — 10
   2.3 What Is Hoshin Kanri? — 11
   2.4 Applying Hoshin Kanri for Selection of LSS Projects — 13
   2.5 Concluding Guidelines — 15

3. Lean Six Sigma Project Selection and Prioritisation — 17
   3.1 Introduction — 17
   3.2 Characteristics of Good and Bad LSS Projects — 18
   3.3 How to Select and Prioritise Projects? — 19
   3.4 Who Is Responsible for Project Selection? — 22
   3.5 Management of Project Reviews — 23
   3.6 Common Reasons for Failure of LSS Projects in Organisations — 25
   3.7 Summary — 27

4. Selecting Top Talent for Execution of Projects — 29
   4.1 Introduction — 29

	4.2 Identifying Top Talent	31
	4.3 Traits of High Potential Employees	33
	4.4 High Potentials in Lean and Six Sigma	34
	4.5 Developing an Agile Program for Lean Six Sigma HiPo Selection	36
	4.6 LSS HiPo Selection Process	36
	4.7 Developing an Agile Program for HiPo in LSS	38
	4.8 Career Progression and Leadership Positions	41
5.	Leadership for Lean Six Sigma Deployment	45
	5.1 Introduction	45
	5.2 Strategic Significance of LSS Leadership	47
	5.3 Essential Leadership Skills for Successful Deployment of LSS	47
	5.4 Leadership Behaviours for LSS Transformation	49
	5.5 Leadership Characteristics for Lean Six Sigma	50
	5.6 Leadership Styles for Lean Six Sigma	53
	5.7 Summary	55
6.	Effective Training and Design of Curriculum for Different LSS Roles	57
	6.1 Introduction	57
	6.2 Lean Six Sigma Curriculum	59
	6.3 LSS Teaching and Training	60
	6.4 Course Preparation	62
	6.5 Soft Skills Training	62
	6.6 Curriculum Development	64
	6.7 Curriculum Assessment	68
	6.8 Challenges, Lesson Learnt and Sustainability	70
	6.9 Summary	71
7.	Development of Rewards and Recognitions for LSS	73
	7.1 Introduction	73
	7.2 Why Rewards and Recognitions?	74
	7.3 Types of Reward and Recognition Systems Effective for LSS	76
	7.4 Rewards and Recognitions – A Management Strategy for Effective Change Management	79
	7.5 Conclusions	80
8.	Lean Six Sigma Sustainability	83
	8.1 Introduction	83
	8.2 Ten Critical Challenges in Sustaining LSS Implementations	84
	8.3 A Few Strategies to Overcome the Challenges of LSS' Sustainability	87
	8.4 Conclusions	89

9. Linking Lean Six Sigma with Innovation and
   Organisational Learning 91
   9.1 Introduction 91
   9.2 Linking LSS with Innovation 92
   9.3 Linking LSS with Organisational Learning 96
   9.4 Summary 99

10. Linking Lean Six Sigma with Green and Environmental
    Sustainability 101
    10.1 Introduction 101
    10.2 Green Lean Six Sigma and Environmental Sustainability 102
    10.3 Challenges and the Emerging Trend of Integration of
         Green Lean Six Sigma 104
    10.4 Conclusions 106

11. Beyond LSS: Emerging Themes of Lean Six Sigma 107
    11.1 Introduction 107
    11.2 Integration of LSS with Robotic Process Automation 108
    11.3 Integration of LSS with Big Data 110
    11.4 LSS within a Holistic Improvement Strategy and
         Methodology 112
    11.5 Integration of LSS with Statistical Engineering 113
    11.6 LSS in Public Sector Organisations 114
    11.7 Integration of LSS into Higher Educational Systems 116

References *117*

Index *129*

LIST OF FIGURES

Figure 2.1	Roadmap to Create Hoshin Kanri X-matrix.	14
Figure 3.1	Effort–Impact Matrix for Project Selection.	20
Figure 4.1	Levels in Lean Six Sigma.	37
Figure 4.2	360-Degree Feedback Mechanism.	40
Figure 4.3	Phase-gate Monitoring.	40
Figure 6.1	Backward Design Process.	65

LIST OF TABLES

Table 3.1	Criteria for Project Selection and Respective Scores.	21
Table 3.2	Criteria and Score for Project Selection.	22
Table 10.1	Linking Lean Green – Similarity in Views.	103

ABOUT THE AUTHORS

Jiju Antony is recognised worldwide as a leader in Lean Six Sigma methodology for achieving and sustaining process excellence. He is a Professor of Quality Management and Director of Process Improvement in the School of Social Sciences at Heriot-Watt University, Edinburgh, Scotland. Professor Antony has been researching on the topic of Six Sigma and Lean Six Sigma since 2001 and published over 200 journal, conference and white papers as well as four books on these two topics alone with over 15,000 citations and H-index of 71; which is considered to be the highest in the world on Operational Excellence topic. He is the founder of the International Conference on Six Sigma and is also the founder of the International Conference on Lean Six Sigma for Higher Education. He is the Editor-in-chief of the *International Journal of Lean Six Sigma*, Associate Editor of the *Total Quality Management & Business Excellence* journal and Associate Editor of *TQM Journal*.

Vijaya Sunder M. is currently Head of Business Process Excellence at the World Bank Group, Chennai. He is a Lean Six Sigma Master Black Belt, PMP, ISO 9001:2015 Quality Lead Auditor, and Lean Facilitator. He holds his PhD in Operational Excellence from the Indian Institute of Technology Madras, a distinction holder in MBA from Sri Sathya Sai Institute of Higher Learning and gold medalist in Bachelor of Engineering from Anna University, India. He has led and mentored various operational excellence programs that helped improve the customer experience, employee satisfaction, eliminate process defects, increase productivity and reduce costs across multinational organisations including World Bank, Barclays, American Express and Citi. He has trained more than 1,500 people (as on July 2018), in Lean Six Sigma, Agile, process automations, strategy and leadership for establishing process improvement capability in firms. Alongside corporate job, he practices teaching for MBA students as a visiting faculty at various business schools and has published research papers in several reputed international journals and magazines.

Chad M. Laux is currently Associate Professor of Computer & Information Technology at Purdue University, West Lafayette, and has developed a concentrated area in Lean Six Sigma where he teaches Lean Six Sigma Systems at the Undergraduate and Graduate levels in Computer & Information Technology. His teaching attracts a wide variety of student majors including Computer & Information Technology, Industrial Engineering Technology, Supply Chain Management Technology, and Healthcare Policy and Management. During his 13 years in the industry, he served primarily in Tier One organisations and managed Quality Engineering, Industrial Engineering and Product Design functions. During that time, Chad received multiple Six Sigma Black Belt certifications and conducted multiple continuous improvement projects.

Elizabeth Cudney is currently Associate Professor in the Engineering Management and Systems Engineering Department at Missouri University of Science and Technology. She received her BS in Industrial Engineering from North Carolina State University, Master of Engineering in Mechanical Engineering and MBA from the University of Hartford, and doctorate in Engineering Management from the University of Missouri – Rolla. In 2018, she received the ASQ Crosby Medal for her book on Design for Six Sigma. She received the 2018 IISE Fellow Award. She also received the 2017 Yoshio Kondo Academic Research Prize from the International Academy for Quality for sustained performance in exceptional published works. She received the 2008 ASQ A.V. Feigenbaum Medal and the 2006 SME Outstanding Young Manufacturing Engineering Award. She has published 9 books and over 85 journal papers. Dr Cudney is a certified Lean Six Sigma Master Black Belt.

PREFACE

Lean Six Sigma (LSS) is a powerful Operational Excellence (OE) methodology for making critical business processes more efficient and effective by reducing waste and variation, which results in enhanced customer satisfaction, improved productivity and reduced operational costs. While the success stories speak for themselves, there were critics who have highlighted the failure of LSS due to various reasons. As more and more organisations are joining the journey of LSS, the failure of this initiative is also surfacing from various organisations. Though there is significant research evidence available on critical success and failure factors of LSS implementation in organisations, these aspects have been merely restricted to the tactical side of LSS.

Though organisations initially realised LSS as an effective toolkit with a collection of problem-solving tools for process improvements, later the evolution of understanding clarified LSS as an organisation strategy and a leadership approach for imbibing the quality culture in organisations. Although a plethora of articles on Lean Six Sigma have been published in a wide variety of sources, the authors have observed that no general guidelines have been provided to organisations for implementing and sustaining this powerful business process improvement strategy.

This book presents *Ten Commandments of Lean Six Sigma* from the perspective of practitioners, researchers and academics who have been involved in the training, teaching, research and consultancy on various topics of quality and continuous improvement such as Lean, Six Sigma and LSS. These commandments can serve as a practical guide for senior managers and executives for achieving operational and service excellence in various manufacturing, service and public sector organisations despite their size. We hope that business executives and senior managers as well as a number of practitioners and consultants will find this book useful in conveying the key elements to launch and sustain an OE journey in any organisational setting.

The book is divided into 11 chapters. The first chapter is an introduction to Lean Six Sigma (LSS) as a powerful Operational Excellence (OE) methodology for achieving both efficiency and effectiveness in business processes. The remaining chapters are the Ten Commandments of Lean Six Sigma which include some of the most important factors which need to be taken into account for the successful journey of LSS. Some chapters include the latest trends or emerging themes which will be essential for the further growth of OE in the next 25 years or so. We truly hope this book inspires many senior managers in organisations to get into the habit of embracing OE strategy for creating and sustaining competitive advantage. We are indebted to many contributors and leading experts for the development of OE strategy and its associated tools and techniques applied in industry today, especially Mr. Taiichi Ohno as the father of the Toyota Production System, Professor James Womack, Professor Daniel Jones and Professor Daniel Roos for their contributions to the Lean Production System in creating value for customers through continuous improvement, Dr. Mikel Harry who has done some pioneering work in Motorola for the development of Six Sigma as a business process improvement strategy and methodology and, finally, Mr. Michael George for his unique contribution to the integration of the most two powerful OE methodologies such as Lean and Six Sigma.

Jiju Antony, Vijaya Sunder M., Chad Laux
and Elizabeth Cudney

ACKNOWLEDGEMENTS

This book was conceived further to publication from an article entitled *Ten Commandments of Lean Six Sigma: a practitioner's perspective* that appeared in the *International Journal of Productivity and Performance Management*. We are deeply indebted to a number of people who, in essence, have made this book what it is today. First, and foremost, we would like to thank a number of colleagues in industry for their constant encouragement in writing up this book. We would like to express our deepest appreciation to Katy Mathers and Pete Baker at Emerald Publishers for their support and forbearance during the course of the project. Finally, we would like to express our sincere thanks to our parents and family for their encouragement and patience as the book stole countless hours away from family activities.

1

INTRODUCTION TO LEAN SIX SIGMA AND TEN COMMANDMENTS

1.1 INTRODUCTION TO LEAN AND SIX SIGMA

While a number of continuous improvement (CI) methodologies exist in the literature, Lean and Sigma have been used for over 30 years in several organisations, proving to be most powerful and renowned. The development of an effective CI strategy is a key factor for long-term success in modern organisations. Over the last 15 years, Lean Six Sigma (LSS) has become one of the most popular and proven business process improvement or CI methodologies organisations have witnessed in the past. This chapter provides a quick overview of Lean, followed by Six Sigma and its integration called LSS. It also outlines the importance of the Ten Commandments of LSS which are primarily aimed for business leaders and senior executives in organisations. The Ten Commandments of LSS are based on several years' experience of four co-authors who act as LSS Master Black Belts, practitioners, trainers and researchers on various topics of Lean, Six Sigma and general quality management/CI topics.

Lean has had a tangential development history compared to Six Sigma. Much of the Lean Production System (LPS) is based on the Toyota Production System (TPS) (Womack, Jones, & Roos, 2007).

TPS has roots that go back to Henry Ford's development of the assembly line and Frederick Taylor's work on scientific management (Womack & Jones, 2003). The concept of LPS involves determining the value of any process in the eyes of customers by distinguishing value-added activities or steps from non-value-added activities or steps and eliminating waste. Krafcik (1988) is generally credited with the first use of the term 'Lean Production System'. Lean began with a manufacturing emphasis and was referred to as lean manufacturing for many years. Gradually, organisations learnt that the same principles of push vs pull system, identification and reduction or even elimination of waste and standardisation of processes/procedures, can also be applied to non-manufacturing settings.

While it is impossible to set a definite date for the beginning of Six Sigma, around the mid-1980s, Bill Smith and his colleagues in Motorola began improvement projects that looked similar to Total Quality Management (TQM). Motorola was facing fierce and stiff competition with its competitors in the pager market and needed to improve quality as well as reduce operational costs to stay in business. Bob Galvin, the CEO of Motorola, along with his colleagues decided to invest in Six Sigma and adopted it as a core strategy at the operational level for delivering quality at low costs. Six Sigma provided an overall roadmap for solving complex problems with unknown solutions (Snee & Hoerl, 2005). Motorola achieved tangible and measurable results to the bottom line, and other organisations began to take notice of Motorola's success including Honeywell (previously Allied Signal). In 1995, Jack Welch who was the CEO of GE (General Electric) stated that the company would incorporate Six Sigma to reduce defects and operational costs. Consequently, this initiative became well recognised, appearing on the front pages of well-known newspapers.

Welch (2001) told Wall Street analysts that Six Sigma would be the biggest initiative ever launched by GE and that it would be his biggest priority for the next five years. Before official results emerged for the company, GE stock began to rise, and many other companies started looking more closely at Six Sigma. Based on GE Capital's success, other financial institutions began Six Sigma initiatives. One of the most successful has been by Bank of America, which has publishing savings in the billions of dollars annually

(Sunder, Ganesh, & Marathe, 2019). Similarly, Commonwealth Health Corporation launched the first major Six Sigma deployment in healthcare in the late 1990s and produced millions of dollars of savings in the radiology department alone within a year (Snee & Hoerl, 2005). In the late 1990s and early 2000s, a large number of organisations, in diverse industries, launched Six Sigma initiatives, including DuPont, Dow Chemical, 3M, Ford and American Express, to name just a few. The US military began major investments in Six Sigma at this time as well. Overseas, companies in Europe and Asia began to implement Six Sigma to varying degrees, particularly Korean companies such as Samsung (Snee & Hoerl, 2003).

1.2 WHY IS THE INTEGRATION OF LEAN AND SIX SIGMA A BETTER APPROACH FOR PROBLEM-SOLVING?

Although both Lean and Six Sigma had produced immense and significant benefits to many organisations, they do have some limitations. George (2002) has successfully integrated these two powerful methodologies for business process improvement and claimed that the integrated approach is superior to using Lean or Six Sigma on its own. His view was that Lean is not well suited to resolving complex problems that require intensive data analysis and advanced statistical tools and techniques. Those implementing Six Sigma found that not every problem needed several months of data collection to resolve. Quality professionals found that Lean principles and tools could be primarily applied with minimal data collection and achieve immediate results.

In many Lean applications, the solution to the problem is known to the team and all that is needed is a methodology and a set of tools to implement the known solution. Lean is primarily focused on the flow of information and material between processes. Therefore, if the root cause of the problem is a flow issue, Lean is likely to work well. However, if the problem involves understanding the most critical process parameters which influence the output and if the output varies significantly due to a number of factors, this will be a great candidate for the Six Sigma methodology.

Deploying Six Sigma in isolation cannot remove all types of waste from the business process, and deploying Lean in isolation cannot bring a process into a state of statistical control and remove variation from the process (Corbett, 2011). Therefore, some companies have decided to merge both methodologies, rather than implement them in isolation to come up with a more powerful strategy for process excellence and optimising processes (Bhuiyan, Baghel, & Wilson, 2006). Bertel (2003) highlighted that using either one of the methodologies alone has limitations: Six Sigma will eliminate defects in processes, but it will not address the question of how to optimise process flow. In contrast, Lean principles are not helpful in achieving high-capability and high-stability processes.

According to Antony, Snee, & Hoerl (2017), the integration of Lean and Six Sigma in organisations increases efficiency and effectiveness, helping them to achieve superior performance faster compared to the implementation of each approach in isolation. Lean Six Sigma (LSS) is a business process improvement methodology that focuses on process performance, resulting in enhanced customer satisfaction and improved bottom-line results in hard-cash savings. LSS provides the concepts, methods, tools and techniques for process management. It is an effective leadership development tool as it prepares leaders for their role in managing change. A review of over 20 case studies of LSS has shown the following benefits of LSS:

- Increased profits and financial savings
- Increased customer satisfaction
- Reduced operational cost
- Reduced cycle time
- Improved key performance metrics
- Reduced defects in processes
- Reduced machine breakdown time
- Reduced inventory
- Improved throughput yield
- Increased production capacity

1.3 LSS METHODOLOGY: AN OVERVIEW

The LSS methodology is used for solving existing problems in any process when the solution is unknown or when a confirmation is needed to validate the root cause of the problem. LSS experts follow a stringent and disciplined methodology called Define-Measure-Analyse-Improve-Control (DMAIC), and this section presents a brief overview of this powerful methodology.

Define Phase: In this phase, we usually define the problem or the opportunity for improvement. This is a very important phase of problem-solving. If we do not define and formulate the problem correctly upfront, one may struggle in the development of appropriate solution at a later stage. The common tools used in this phase are Voice of the Customer (VOC) analysis, Supplier–Input–Process–Output–Customer (SIPOC), Process Mapping, Project Charter, etc.

Measure Phase: In this phase, we need to measure the baseline performance of the process, and this measurement is used as a yardstick for further improvement. The common tools used in this phase are Critical-to-Quality drill-down tree, Measurement System Analysis (MSA), Run Charts or Control Charts, Process Capability Analysis, etc.

Analyse Phase: In this phase, we need to understand the potential/root causes of the problem due to excessive process variability. Typical tools used in this phase include Hypothesis Testing, Pareto Chart, Scatter Diagram, Correlation Analysis, Cause and Effect Analysis, Histogram, Root Cause Analysis, etc.

Improve Phase: In this phase, the process performance will be improved through the development of potential solutions which can eliminate the root causes of the problem at hand. One may generate potential solutions, select and prioritise them, perform risk assessment, pilot the solution for its effectiveness and finally evaluate the benefits. Typical tools used in this phase include Prioritisation Matrix, Design of Experiments, Single Minute Exchange of Dies, etc.

Control Phase: The goal of the control step is to sustain the gains by standardising the work methods or processes, anticipating future improvements and capturing and documenting the key lessons learnt from the project and exploring the opportunities of transferring the knowledge to other operations in the business. Typical tools used in this phase include Standard Operating Procedures (SOP), Visual Management, Control Charts, Poka-Yoke (Mistake-Proofing), etc.

1.4 AN OVERVIEW OF THE TEN COMMANDMENTS OF LSS

In this section, the authors provide an outline of the Ten Commandments of LSS. These are the essential ingredients to be understood by senior executives and business leaders in any organisational setting for the successful deployment of LSS. Each chapter in the book will be focussing on these vital points in detail.

1. **Alignment of Lean Six Sigma with organisational strategy:** The leaders and business executives should ensure that the LSS is an integral part of the organisational strategy and ensure that selection of projects is aligned with the strategic goals of the business.

2. **Lean Six Sigma project selection and prioritisation:** For the successful journey of LSS and its sustainability, it is essential that projects must be identified and prioritised for their execution by project teams.

3. **Selecting the top talent for the execution of projects:** In order to gain momentum for the use of LSS in any organisation, it is critical that one should select the top talented people for the execution of projects and a set of skills should be developed for project leaders at Green Belt and Black Belt levels.

4. **Leadership for LSS:** Leadership has proved to be one of the most critical success factors of LSS (Laureani & Antony, 2018). Deming suggested that quality excellence could not be achieved in organisations without educating leadership on the

importance of quality, and the same analogy could be applied to process excellence.

5. **Effective training and design of curriculum for different LSS roles:** Training should be imparted to all those concerned such as LSS project champions and LSS project leader (Black Belts, Green Belts, etc). An awareness of LSS through LSS executive workshops is highly desirable for all senior managers in the organisation to understand their level of involvement and commitment throughout the implementation and sustainability of LSS.

6. **Development of reward and recognition system:** A reward and recognition system should be an inherent part of any change management initiative. Leaders in the organisation should introduce some form of incentive or reward and recognition system for sustainability of the LSS initiative.

7. **Lean Six Sigma sustainability:** Sustainability of LSS is one of the biggest challenges for all organisations today. The authors suggest the importance of sustainability in the roadmap of successful LSS deployment and people should be aware of the factors which influence the sustainability of the LSS initiative.

8. **Linking LSS with organisational learning and innovation:** LSS is an enabler of individual learning as it promotes activity-based learning though project management and structured problem-solving. Anand, Ward, Tatikonda, & Schilling (2009) provides empirical evidence of the dynamic capability perspective and its underlying theory of organisational learning for CI such as LSS. A study carried out by Antony, Setijono, & Dahlgaard (2016) with 10 UK-based companies has shown that LSS fosters continuous or incremental innovation.

9. **Linking LSS with Green and environmental sustainability:** Recent research suggests that Lean, Six Sigma and Green approaches make a positive contribution to the economic, social and environmental (i.e. sustainability) performance of organisations. The results of one study showed that the

integration of LSS and Green helped the organisations to reduce their resources consumption on average by 30% and minimise the cost of energy and mass streams by 9% on average (Cherrafi et al., 2017).

10. **Beyond Lean Six Sigma:** Research has shown that several themes have emerged over the past few years which are complementary to LSS. These themes are derived from authors' interventions with a few companies as well as involvement of several panel discussions and interactive workshops from various conferences the authors have been involved with. These themes include LSS and Big Data, LSS and Industry 4.0, LSS and Rapid Process Automation. Business leaders and senior executives should have a solid understanding of these emerging themes and, consequently, integrate these methodologies within their organisations.

1.5 SUMMARY

This chapter provides an overview of the book clearly outlining the origin of LPS, the origin of Six Sigma and then demonstrating the importance of the integration of Lean with Six Sigma or LSS. This chapter also outlines the Ten Commandments of Lean Six Sigma and how these commandments can be beneficial to senior business leaders and executives in organisations, irrespective of their size and nature.

2

ALIGNMENT OF LEAN SIX SIGMA WITH ORGANISATIONAL STRATEGY

2.1 INTRODUCTION

This chapter emphasises the need for alignment of the Lean Six Sigma strategy with the organisational strategy that emerges from its vision and goals. It is important for this alignment as its absence could lead to Lean Six Sigma efforts getting wasted due to lack of direction. Organisational strategy when aligned with the Lean Six Sigma strategy not only provides direction across all levels in the organisation but also helps realise higher returns on investments from Lean Six Sigma initiatives. A strategy deployment tool known as Hoshin Kanri is discussed in this chapter for this effect. Companies that use Hoshin Kanri often follow a process, which is comparable to W. Edwards Deming's Plan-Do-Check-Act cycle. The Hoshin X-matrix that systematically aligns the long-term objectives of the organisation to the actionable target items is discussed with examples. The three main applications of using Hoshin process as part of strategy deployment include (1) measuring the organisational system as a whole, (2) setting a future state, (3) including everyone in the organisation to realise the future state. The application of Hoshin Kanri towards identifying the Lean Six Sigma projects is highlighted in this chapter. The outcome of the

Hoshin Kanri activity that leads to specific, actionable Lean Six Sigma project opportunities for execution and governance, is presented here as a resource for Lean Six Sigma practitioners and aspiring organisational leaders.

2.2 NEED FOR ALIGNING LSS WITH ORGANISATIONAL STRATEGY

Organisational strategy is a dynamic long-term plan that helps realise a company's goals and vision. So, it is natural to align a company's investments in line with their strategies. In fact, any investments that a company makes towards building a culture should be guided by its strategies. Lean Six Sigma is a culture building vehicle for imbibing quality excellence, and hence it is essential to align it with the organisational strategy. It needs to be viewed as a mindset and strategic initiative rather than a tactical approach.

Significant investments are made by organisations during LSS deployment. Further, participative leadership, continuous improvement and total employee participation enable bottom-line benefits and a culture of quality excellence. Therefore, it is important to view LSS deployment from a strategic lens. Hence, active participation of senior management is essential to the success of Lean Six Sigma within any organisation irrespective of its industry, nature or size. But, it is equally important for the top leadership's outcomes, especially the organisational strategy, to flow top-down seamlessly. Without this top-down flow of organisation strategy, the energies of employees will work in all different directions, with no process ownership which leads to waste of resources.

In our experience working on several improvement programs across various multinational firms, we have realised that without its alignment with the organisational strategy, a continuous improvement initiative cannot succeed, and Lean Six Sigma is not an exception. The first step for an organisation to get ready for Lean Six Sigma deployment is to communicate top-down, 'what' a company wants to achieve (its vision and goals) and 'how' it wants to achieve (mission and strategy) through Six Sigma. This is where aligning organisational strategy to Lean Six Sigma strategy becomes essential. In absence of such an alignment, there is a high possibility of failing to select the right people and right projects for the Lean Six Sigma deployment. For example, if a company's strategy is 'realise cost efficiencies', then the appropriate Lean Six Sigma strategy should be to identify projects that would potentially result in lowering the cost of resources (human, financial, infrastructure, etc.). But, if the company's strategy is to 'increase sales of existing products', then the Lean Six Sigma strategy should be different. Hence, devising a Lean Six Sigma strategy is important to establish a clear roadmap or path on the journey of quality excellence; and it is equally important to align the Lean Six Sigma strategy to the larger organisational strategy. Therefore, in summary, managers should align company goals (strategy) with the plans of middle management (tactics), work performed by employees (operations) and projects for improvement of operations in order to build a culture of quality excellence (Lean Six Sigma) and ensure that everyone is moving in the same direction at the same time.

2.3 WHAT IS HOSHIN KANRI?

Hoshin Kanri (management by policy) is a powerful technique for ensuring that the strategic goals of a company drive the progress and actions at every level within that company. Lean Six Sigma is best deployed into an organisation's strategy when it becomes part of 'how to deploy' the strategy. In this process, it becomes easier to classify and differentiate projects into short-term and long-term, high priority and low priority, low impact and high impact towards the firm's strategy, etc.

Hoshin Kanri is a Japanese management term which means direction (Ho), focus (shin), alignment (kan) and reason (ri). It prescribes four key elements for the above stated purpose namely, vision, policy development, policy deployment and policy control. Hoshin Kanri-based management is unique and reflects the personality of the organisation almost from the start. The approach was originally developed in Japan in the 1960s and first introduced to in the West in a text translated from the Japanese and edited by Yoji Akao (1991). Several organisations today follow Hoshin Kanri with different names. For example, AT&T and Texas Instruments call it policy deployment; at Hewlett-Packard and Proctor & Gamble, it's labelled hoshin planning; Xerox Corporation calls it managing for results and at Unilever, it's management into action.

What makes Hoshin Kanri unique from other strategy formulation and implementation methodologies is its application of quality excellence right from the policy level. In other words, it is as simple as translating the quality mindset into cascading objectives and subsequent actions at all levels and to all processes. This process happens in conjunction with a full use of quality tools to gather information, identify issues, prioritise critical actions and implement solutions, enabling the organisation to achieve the right position in the marketplace.

There are four sequential steps to implement Hoshin Kanri that are briefly explained below:

1. **Establishing vision:** First, the leadership of the company should develop a strong vision by answering the question 'Why does the company exist?' Second, the leadership team should define key objectives or a mission. These are the 'hows', if achieved, they will create a competitive edge for the company.

2. **Policy development:** At this stage, the leadership team along with the senior managers breaks down the objectives into annual goals. Then, organisational policies get developed in such a way that they enable an organisation to meet the annual goals. This is an important step in the Hoshin Kanri process, as the policies that get developed in this stage will determine the path of deployment in the later stages.

3. **Policy deployment:** Once the annual goals are crafted, they are 'deployed' across all levels of the organisation. This is the process of 'goal setting' which starts at the top and is propagated to each employee. Then, the real execution starts where all energies of the workforce work unidirectionally to achieve the set goals.

4. **Policy control:** The monthly reviews make sure that the policy is being executed according to the plan. At the end of the year, there will be an annual review, which validates the results that have been achieved. The lessons learnt in a year flow to the next year's policy development process, and the iterative feedback loop ensures ongoing organisational learning.

The next section explains how to use the above-said Hoshin Kanri for the selection of Lean Six Sigma projects in organisations.

2.4 APPLYING HOSHIN KANRI FOR SELECTION OF LSS PROJECTS

While applying Hoshin Kanri in the context of identifying Lean Six Sigma projects, it is advised that it is not executed strictly top-down, as in case of other organisational initiatives. While the strategies and long-term goals remain top-down, setting the short-term objectives should be a joint effort between a manager and their team to mutually agree on the optimal set of goals and associated actions. This is the unique feature of Lean Six Sigma that balances both top-down and bottom-up approaches for effective change management. This process, otherwise referred to as 'catchball' enables employees at all levels to be engaged in the strategic planning process in their own capacities and also promotes a feeling of employee empowerment which is an essential component of drawing employee participation (Tennant & Roberts, 2001). The benefit of involving staff in setting the short-term objectives in the context of Lean Six Sigma will actively work as it creates a sense of belongingness that they will think through the process details much more thoroughly. In fact, it is the staff who knows the processes better than anyone else in the organisation, and naturally it is in their minds where process improvement ideas take shape.

The first step in applying Hoshin Kanri for identifying Lean Six Sigma projects is to create a Hoshin Kanri 'X-matrix'. In our experience of using the X-matrix, we found it to be a great way to put things together for everyone to easily understand and refer to for what needs to be accomplished and by when. The X-matrix classifies the Lean Six Sigma vision into two objective parts: long-term and short-term. These terms are generally subjective and are based on individual organisation's decision of what should be a short/long. For example, a short-term objective could be to improve customer satisfaction, and long term to sustain the improved customer satisfaction. Based on the long- and short-term objectives that are set at organisational level, the year's annual objectives get set at the functional level. Every objective will be associated with a critical metric to improve. For example, in the above case the metric to improve is 'customer satisfaction score'. Each of these metrics is then rehabilitated into Lean Six Sigma project opportunities with specific project level goals. Continuing with this example, a possible goal could be 'to improve the customer satisfaction score from 85% to 95% by end of the year'.

Fig. 2.1 illustrates a roadmap of the Hoshin Kanri X-matrix. The first step in making the X-matrix is to determine the long-term goals at the organisation level. These are derived from the vision and strategy which clarify the purpose and the aspiring future state. Thus, the long-term objectives determine the 'What' to be achieved. Based on the set long-term objectives, the short-term or annual objectives are developed. These help determine 'How Far' to achieve this year? In the matrix between the long-term objectives and the

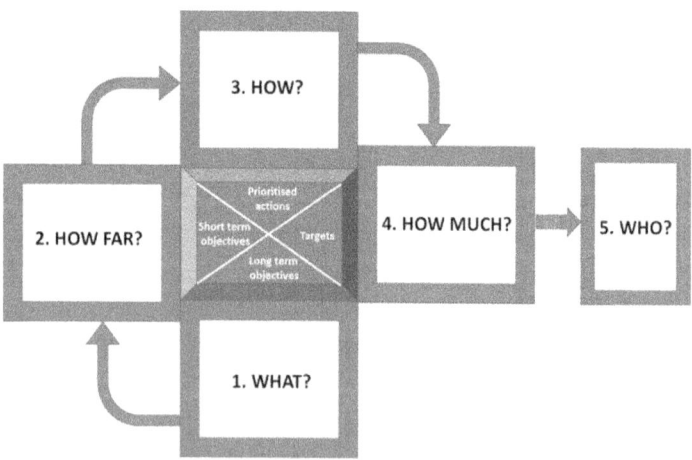

Fig. 2.1. Roadmap to Create Hoshin Kanri X-matrix.

annual objectives, you mark which long-term objective is aligned with which annual objective. It is at this stage the staff members are involved in determining the short-term objectives. Then, as a third step, between manager and staff, discussions should emerge the list of actions that will determine 'How' to achieve the set short-term goals. These actions should reflect the new initiatives that the teams have to commence or improve upon the success of the existing initiatives. For example, an action item could be to start an employee ideation initiative through crowdsourcing within the organisation. This action should help achieve ways to improve the short-term goal of improving customer satisfaction. Upon successful identification of the actions to meet the short-term goals, the list is prioritised by senior management based on each action's alignment with the long-term goals. For each of these prioritised actions, specific targets are set by managers in consultation with the staff. Thus, this stage of the X-matrix determines 'How Much' to achieve from the actions set. Each of these target items represents a Lean Six Sigma project. The far right of Fig. 2.1 shows 'Who' will be responsible for implementation of these actions (preferably Lean Six Sigma project leaders). This way the X-matrix is completed by determining the responsibilities for the set actions.

2.5 CONCLUDING GUIDELINES

Hoshin Kanri requires a strategic vision in order to succeed. The strategic or long-term objectives that emerge from the vision help craft the short-term or annual objectives. But this is not a onetime annual activity. While the big goals are fixed, they need to be broken down into smaller goals, on a weekly and monthly basis, and then implemented so that everyone, from management to the front-line staff, is in agreement on what needs to be accomplished. The actions that emerge from the short-term goals and their targets together represent the Lean Six Sigma project opportunities in organisations. But, not all targets that emerge out of a Hoshin Kanri X-matrix deserve to be taken up as Lean Six Sigma projects. Please refer to project prioritisation using effort-impact matrix discussed in Chapter 3.

The progress of these actions against their set targets should be reviewed periodically. This project governance is important as every project success ties back to the long-term objectives and vision of the organisation. On completion of every phase of the Lean Six Sigma project, a tollgate review meeting is suggested. Similarly, at the end of every Lean Six Sigma project the benefits realised should be aligned with the set objectives, and the satisfaction of these objectives should be reviewed on a monthly basis, with a larger annual review at the end of the year. Performance measurement and governance should be a key part of the process.

Traditionally, Hoshin Kanri is a top-down approach, with the goals being mandated by management and the implementation being performed by employees. However, including staff in setting the short-term goals and subsequent actions as a catchball process helps in change management. As such, catchball is often used in order to aid in the execution of the strategic plan and to get opinions of both managers and employees through meetings and interactions in order to ensure the bidirectional flow of goals, feedback and other information throughout the organisation.

3

LEAN SIX SIGMA PROJECT SELECTION AND PRIORITISATION

3.1 INTRODUCTION

This chapter provides an overview of how to select and prioritise projects when organisations pursue a Lean Six Sigma (LSS) journey. However, the authors noticed that there has been confusion amongst many senior managers in organisations regarding when LSS projects should be executed. It is vital to note that Lean Six Sigma projects are implemented when solutions to problems are unknown at the outset of a problem-solving exercise. Nevertheless, this does not imply that when the solutions are known, projects are easy to execute in organisations. For instance, implementation of a new IT system across a department does not require the application of Lean Six Sigma methodology as the solution is known at the outset. Examples of 'solution unknown' projects include reducing the errors in an invoicing process, decreasing the number of defects in a manufacturing assembly operation, increasing the throughput yield of a process, reducing the variation in turnaround times for cataract surgery in a hospital setting and so on. In these cases, the root causes of the problem are either unknown or vaguely known to the problem-solving team. For problems of such nature, one may have to collect data and perform statistical analyses to understand the root causes and then decide what actions to take. Many practitioners of Lean Six Sigma argue that Lean projects are 'solution known' because they typically involve applying known, proven principles instead of discovering an unknown solution (Snee & Hoerl, 2018). This does not mean Lean projects are easier to execute as tools, principles and basic concepts need to be applied to particular processes where the problems lie. The focus of this chapter is on 'solution-unknown' projects using LSS and how to select and prioritise such projects in organisations.

3.2 CHARACTERISTICS OF GOOD AND BAD LSS PROJECTS

As significant investment in terms of time and resources are required for the execution of LSS projects, it is essential to understand the characteristics of good LSS projects to be executed by either Green Belts (GBs) or Black Belts (BBs) in many organisations. The senior management team should ensure that an appropriate environment is created for result-oriented teamwork. The senior management team should also provide the right support and encouragement to the project leaders and team, from project selection to completion. In our experience, the following are some of the characteristics of good LSS projects, and these may be used as general guidelines in the selection of LSS projects.

- The problem must be aligned with the strategic objectives of the business and hence a business priority to senior managers.
- The solution to the problem should clearly demonstrate a major improvement in business process performance (e.g. a minimum of 25%).
- The solution to the problem should demonstrate a major financial improvement in hard cash savings (e.g. a minimum of $100k).
- The time to completion of the project should be between four and six months.
- The baseline metrics associated with the problem should be well defined.
- The problem under investigation should have the support of the senior management team.

One should also understand the characteristics of bad LSS projects associated with a given problem under investigation. If the project under consideration falls into any of the following classifications, the authors strongly recommend either avoiding or revisiting the problem area and hence project scope further.

- Objectives of the project are fuzzy
- No or poor metrics associated with the problem
- Project is not tied to hard cash savings
- Scope is too broad or narrow (e.g. save the planet project)
- Lack of project alignment with corporate strategic objectives
- No data available to support the problem at hand
- No dedicated LSS project champion for the project
- Lack of resources or inadequate resources
- Selection of pet projects

3.3 HOW TO SELECT AND PRIORITISE PROJECTS?

Before the selection of projects, it is a good idea to work out a strategy for LSS project selection. This should address two important questions: who will be involved in the selection of the project and how the projects will be selected. Instead of individuals selecting a project, it is better to form a team for the finalisation of projects. This team can consist of top management members and project champions/sponsors. The process owners of the respective processes also can be included in the team. The presence of top management is essential as they understand the priority of the organisation better than anyone else. It is beneficial to include a representative of the finance/accounts department in this team. Their involvement will be helpful with the estimation of financial benefits from the LSS projects, as they understand the language of money better (Kumar, Antony, & Cho, 2009).

When the projects are selected, generally two approaches can be followed. The top management team can select a project and assign it to the LSS project team for execution, or the LSS project teams can identify a project and approach top management for approval. In either case, the ultimate authority for approval of the project is with top management. The authors will be presenting two simple methods for the selection of LSS projects in this chapter. The first method is based on a simple effort–impact matrix and the second one is based on the criteria-based project prioritisation matrix. In a typical effort–impact matrix approach, one may try to estimate the effort in completing a project and its impact (measured in terms of benefits) for the organisation. A typical impact might include cost reduction, cost avoidance, increase in customer satisfaction scores, on-time delivery, or increase in process yield. In this case, the effort involves the resources (manpower, budgetary support, etc.) and the support needed from senior management for the successful completion of the project. A typical form of effort–impact matrix is presented in Fig. 3.1. There are four possible combinations based on the 'high' and 'low' values of effort and impact. The initial focus of the projects should be low in effort but high on impact. This is to gain the attention of senior managers and demonstrate the power of LSS as a problem-solving methodology.

The second method for selecting the projects is based on a set of criteria. These criteria should be determined as a pre-requisite exercise, with input from various team members who are involved in process improvement activities across the organisation.

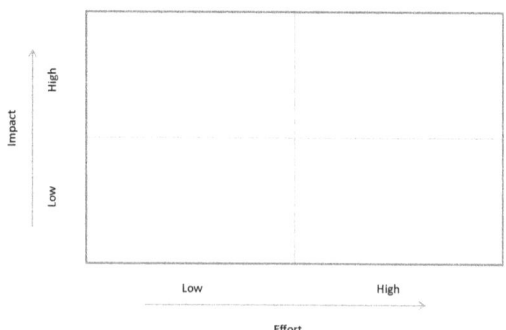

Fig. 3.1. Effort–Impact Matrix for Project Selection.

Each criterion is given a weighting of 1–10 (1 = least important and 10 = most important). Each project is mapped against the chosen criteria, and each participant is asked if the selected project has any link with the set criteria and to rate this on a scale of 1 (project has no link with a particular criterion) to 9 (project has very strong link with a particular criterion). The possible criteria which may be considered for the selection of LSS projects (this is an example only) are:

- Strategic alignment of projects with business or corporate strategic objectives (labelled as 'strategic alignment' in Table 3.1).
- Contribute to measurable and quantifiable financial savings to the bottom line (labelled as 'financial savings' in Table 3.1).
- Impact on customer satisfaction (labelled as 'customer satisfaction' in Table 3.1)
- Completion of projects within four to six months (labelled as 'time' in Table 3.1).
- Risks associated with the project due to the nature of complexity (labelled as 'risk' in Table 3.1).
- Linking LSS with employee satisfaction (labelled as 'employee satisfaction').

Table 3.1. Criteria for Project Selection and Respective Scores.

Criteria	Score
Strategic alignment	10
Financial savings	9
Customer satisfaction	9
Time	8
Risk	8
Employee satisfaction	5

Table 3.2. Criteria and Score for Project Selection.

Projects	Strategic Alignment (10)	Financial Savings (9)	Customer Satisfaction (9)	Time (8)	Risk (8)	Employee Satisfaction (5)	Total Score
Project 1	3	5	8	4	5	1	224
Project 2	5	5	6	6	7	3	268
Project 3	6	7	4	5	4	2	241
Project 4	8	8	7	3	4	4	**291**
Project 5	4	5	5	7	8	4	270

Once the criteria and the respective scores are finalised, the team along with the LSS champion identifies projects from various processes across the business. Each project is ranked against each criterion and the values are written in the corresponding cell. Finally, a total weighted score is calculated for each project as shown in Table 3.2. For example, the first project is not strongly aligned to strategic objectives and the team assigned a score of 3, it can demonstrate reasonable savings to the bottom line and hence assigned a score of 5, clearly linked to customer satisfaction and hence assigned a score of 8, can be completed within the timescale of five months and hence assigned a score of 4, has a medium risk associated with the project and therefore assigned a score of 5 and very little to do employee satisfaction and hence assigned a score of 1. The total score for this project is calculated as $(10 \times 3) + (9 \times 5) + (9 \times 8) + (8 \times 4) + (8 \times 5) + (5 \times 1) = 224$. The last column in Table 3.2 provides the total weighted score for each project. Project 4 has the highest score and therefore should be selected as the best candidate (further to consultation with the LSS project champion and team members).

3.4 WHO IS RESPONSIBLE FOR PROJECT SELECTION?

When organisations launch a Lean Six Sigma initiative, the selection of the first wave or second wave of projects is clearly a non-delegable role for senior management team. The senior management team should have a dedicated role in the selection of projects to ensure that projects are tied to strategic objectives of the business and moreover they should be linked to both the Voice of the Customer (VOC) and Voice of the Business (VOB). Some organisations involve their BBs in selecting projects. However, in our experience, many BBs do not have a good understanding of the strategic priorities of the business and hence the projects should be discussed with the senior management team to determine which are worthy of the available resources.

Many middle-level managers who are qualified BBs in organisations allocate resources to their pet projects. This is a common problem across many organisations today, and therefore the project selection process should be carried out with a number of people including the senior management team, LSS project champion, subject matter experts (BBs, GBs, etc.) as well as project stakeholders. Many LSS BBs often do not have sufficient exposure to high-level business issues, and therefore many have a somewhat myopic perspective on the project selection process (Bertels, 2003).

3.5 MANAGEMENT OF PROJECT REVIEWS

As with every project, regular reviews are crucial to ensure that LSS projects will deliver the anticipated results. Senior management team members will be involved in the review process to identify the stumbling blocks and potential pitfalls associated with the projects. Moreover, regular reviews also enable the LSS project champion and team members in learning problem-solving methodologies, potential barriers to the successful completion of the project and sharing some of the rudimentary challenges in the execution and timely completion.

LSS project champions have a huge role to play in the success or failure in the project. Although their role is not to solve the problem, they have to facilitate problem-solving through regular interactions with the LSS project leader (usually a LSS BB or GB) and team members. Champions in many cases encourage creative thinking and challenge the team, while making sure that the project is on track and achieves its goals in the given timeline.

Additionally, they ensure that the team has access to the necessary resources allocated to complete the project and then communicate its success across the business via monthly newsletters or other similar means.

Two types of reviews must be performed for each LSS project. The first type of review is completed by an individual from top management along with an LSS project champion, and the second type of review is by the LSS expert who is an experienced MBB or BB with supervision of various projects. The focus of the first type of review is to gauge the overall progress of the project with respect to project objectives, project timeline and its alignment with business objectives. The exact format of the review is not essential; however, the review takes place at each stage of the problem-solving phase of the methodology (Define–Measure–Analyse–Improve–Control (DMAIC)). The following questions can be concluded as checkpoints during the review by champion (Antony, Vinodh, & Gijo, 2016):

- Is the project executed per the planned schedule?
- Are team members able to provide the time required for the project?
- Is the overall progress made in the specific phase of DMAIC acceptable?
- Is there a problem with respect to budget and resources?
- Are there any perceived risks associated with the project?

The review by the LSS expert should be focused on the application of tools and techniques being utilised in each phase of the problem. Moreover, the data collection strategy, analysis of data and interpretation of key findings are the main focus during this review. The following questions can be used as checkpoints during the review by the LSS expert:

- Is the project addressing all important steps in different phases of the problem-solving methodology?
- Is the plan for data collection appropriate and sound?

- How correctly is the analysis being performed? Are the right tools being used at the right stage of the methodology for analysis?
- Are the conclusions from each phase or stage of the methodology and the resulting actions appropriate?
- Are there good control measures in place for sustaining the improved performance?
- Who will be the process owner after the completion of the project and what are the roles and responsibilities of the process owner?

3.6 COMMON REASONS FOR FAILURE OF LSS PROJECTS IN ORGANISATIONS

Project selection is one of the critical factors in the success of any business change programme, whether it is short-term or long-term. Identification of high-impact projects at the initial stage of a programme will result in significant breakthroughs in a rapid timeframe. A critical point for sustainability of Lean Six Sigma efforts in any organisation is to select the right project from the outset, as this determines the success or failure of the deployment of Six Sigma. Brice (2002) stated that most projects fall behind schedule or fail, due to a tenuous linkage of these projects to the organisation's strategic business goals. The following are some of the common reasons for failure of LSS projects:

- **Poorly scoped projects, which typically attempt to 'boil the ocean' or 'save the planet':** Proper scoping of the project with the right team members as well as frequent project reviews can target some of the scoping issues at early stages of the project.
- **Choice of inappropriate improvement methodology for the problem at hand:** No single methodology can tackle all the business problems in any organisation. The choice of a suitable methodology depends upon the nature of the problem one is trying to solve.

- **Lack of involvement of top management from project selection to completion of projects:** Choose projects which have full support and commitment of top management as this would give a strong signal to the entire organisation about the priority of the project.

- **Insufficient time given to the project leader and team members:** One of the major challenges for many people who have attended LSS training courses was that they have not been given sufficient time for completing the project due to other priorities in their businesses. This is one of the reasons we strongly recommend the use of an LSS project champion to tackle problems of this nature.

- **Selection of the right people for the execution of a project:** Selection of appropriate team members plays an important role in the success of the LSS project. People who are highly capable of managing change within the organisation with an eagerness to learn and implement new ideas, are to be included in the team.

- **Lack of available data to understand the problem:** In our experience with the project selection process, we encourage choosing the initial wave of projects with medium to high availability of data.

- **Sub-optimal team size and composition:** The Lean Six Sigma project team should have four to six members. As the size of the team increases, it becomes difficult to find mutually agreeable meeting times and to reach group consensus. More importantly, the composition of a project team is a critical element to decide. There should be adequate representation from relevant functional units. Though diversity in a team is a much-needed feature, members should be given enough time to understand each other's personality for better team cohesion (Antony & Gupta, 2019).

- **Inappropriate rewards and recognition system/culture:** Introduction of appropriate rewards and recognition schemes in the organisation can motivate people to come forward and take up more LSS projects. The incentive or reward system fosters a sense of achievement and company recognition, thus generating greater employee motivation and commitment in future improvement projects, producing a spiral effect (Ho, Chang, & Wang, 2008). Rewards and recognition systems also maintain a positive attitude amongst employees and raise morale, which in turn leads to higher productivity and performance at both individual and organisational levels.

- **Lack of monitoring and control:** Monitoring and control in project management is an important factor for setting the pace for process improvement projects by a process expert and a process improvement project champion. Monitoring systems should be designed and developed to track the on-time progression of a project. The monitoring system reports should be disseminated using visual management tools at workplace seminars and meetings in order to create awareness amongst members and for the purpose of corrective actions which may be required.

- **Resistance to change (partial cooperation by employees):** The implementation of a Lean Six Sigma program involves a change in the existing culture and the acceptance of a new culture for top management and all other employees in the organisation. The authors recommend that management identify potential causes of employees' resistance to change and take appropriate action by developing strategies in sustaining a positive culture.

3.7 SUMMARY

The identification and selection of the right projects and right people or team for the project within the LSS still remains a challenging task, and many organisations continue to struggle. Poor project selection continues to happen surprisingly often, even in the best-managed and best-performing organisations, and this can undermine the success and credibility of the Lean Six Sigma program. This chapter provides an overview about LSS projects explicitly covering the points such as what constitutes a good LSS project, how to select and prioritise LSS projects, people who are responsible for project selection and their roles and responsibilities, how to manage project reviews effectively and finally common reasons for failures of LSS projects.

4

SELECTING TOP TALENT FOR EXECUTION OF PROJECTS

4.1 INTRODUCTION

Hiring is the most important decision that an organisation makes. As an organisation grows, success depends on the organisational workforce. Becker, Huselid, and Beatty (2009) state that a workforce 'is the most expensive yet poorly managed asset in most organizations'. The best possible method for getting top talent is a significant question to answer for any organisation. According to Brian Tracy (Macleod, 2018), 'As a business owner or manager, you know that hiring the wrong person is the costliest mistake you can make'. During the research for this chapter, numerous articles and cases were reviewed related to hiring of right talent, including an unconventional recruitment campaign – 'The Candidate' undertaken by Heineken to hire the right talent for their organisation (Radic, 2013). Heineken went out of its way to hire the right candidate, and their novel hiring style may have set a benchmark in recruitment worthy of LSS discussion.

It was 2013, the Champions League was approaching, and Heineken posted a job for hiring an intern for its event and sponsorship marketing team. Heineken received 1,734 applications for this one position. Heineken wanted to hire the right candidate for this job and, therefore, followed an unconventional method to test applicants. The aim of the recruitment campaign was to assess the short-listed applicants' personality in terms of attitude, wit and presence of mind. Therefore, applicants were made to undergo three unusual situations. In the first situation, the boss led an interviewee to a meeting room while holding their hand the entire way. The second situation tested the applicant's medical assistance skills through a scenario that involved assisting to revive from a blackout situation during the interview. Finally, the third situation tested the applicant's emergency preparedness through a fire drill, which involved the fire-fighter team calling for help to rescue a stranded employee from the top of the building after a fire alarm. The entire recruitment process was filmed secretly, and the top three finalists were identified, with the most voted candidate making it to the final list. That video soon went viral, and Heineken was recognised as an innovator and trend-setter in the field of recruitment (Radic, 2013).

Globalisation has made the business environment complex and much more stressful. Businesses are experiencing a transition in their vision and mission. Early in the nineteenth century, during the industrial revolution, the focus of business was to manufacture products with a focus on sales as the key to sustainability, growth and expansion. Gradually, the business environment changed, and focus shifted from sales to marketing. Businesses became more customer-centric and quality focused. In an effort to deliver the best customer service and quality, businesses required trained personnel as professionals; therefore, human resource management emerged as an important corporate dimension in the twenty-first century.

Talent management is one of the critical success factors (CSFs) for human resource management. Management of talent has found an important place in the modern knowledge economy as the focus of businesses is to create, deliver and manage knowledge. Selecting, nurturing and retaining talent is key to success and growth for any business (Baedecke Yllner & Brunila, 2013).

A marker of the importance of talent management in the corporate world was after McKinsey & Company published an article, 'War for Talents' (Chambers, Foulon, Handfield-Jones, Hankin, & Michaels, 1998). The article highlights the difficulty of identifying and retaining talent. The study surveyed 77 companies from a variety of industries, and one of the most important findings found was 'companies are more focused on management of financial and physical assets'. Executive talent was the most undermanaged corporate asset from the 1980s and 1990s. The article also discussed that hiring the right talent was easier than retaining personnel; therefore, companies were required to formulate a winning employee value proposition to identify and retain talent. The publication of 'War for Talent' was eye-opening for many and today, human resources are a key for organisational success.

Patel (2017), the CEO of WebProfits, published an article in *Inc.* magazine where Patel discusses prominent challenges that recruiters are facing across the globe. A primary challenge that Patel mentions is identifying the quality candidates, which has always been and continues to challenge firms. With customer expectations changing frequently, companies need to train their employees to address new customer requirements, and that requires time. Therefore, finding the right fit for every required position requires time for transition, training or hiring of new personnel (Cudney & Keim, 2017). A gap will persist, and the only way to bridge the gap between talent placement and the work is to identify talent that already exists by developing strategies to identify and retain top talent. The war for talent may never end; therefore, organisations need to develop strategies to identify future star employees and develop their potential for acquiring leadership positions in the future.

4.2 IDENTIFYING TOP TALENT

The idea of formulating organisational success is not a new one. Daniel (1961) describes the importance of contextual factors for business success as a set of environmental conditions. A strategy for identifying CSFs as business requirements, prior to the adoption of strategy was refined by Bullen, Rockart, and No (1981). Their research argued that the measurement of management strategy could be defined and improved through the identification and adoption of CSFs. Research linking CSFs to successful business strategy is abundant in the literature (Brotherton & Leslie, 1991; Devlin, 1989; Ketelhohn, 1998; Laux, Johnson, & Cada, 2015; Leidecker & Bruno, 1984).

Identifying top talent is a CSF for organisational growth. The identification of top talent refers to the identification of employees who are deemed high potential (HiPo). HiPo individuals are identified and marked as future leaders of their representative businesses and industry. According to Schumacher (2009), HiPos are the individuals who consistently deliver extraordinary performance by engaging themselves in the organisational processes and demonstrating their expertise in achieving organisational goals. Hiring top talent is a crucial step as the quality of LSS project execution depends on the skills and abilities of the people working in LSS (Antony, Gupta, Sunder, & Gijo, 2018).

The HiPo employee has a proven high-performance track record with three distinguishing attributes. These attributes serve as a foundation for HiPos to rise to critical top-level roles (CEB, 2014):

1. Aspiration – This is the attribute that each HiPo must possess. Aspiration refers to the individual's inherent desire to rise in the ladder of career growth. These individuals possess an intrinsic motivation to perform extraordinarily on any job.

2. Ability – Employees should demonstrate a high degree of knowledge, skills and abilities to perform the given task and deliver the desired output. This is an important attribute required to handle senior level roles.

3. Engagement – This refers to the talent of an employee to get along with organisational changes, welcome challenging tasks and deliver the required output (SHL Talent Measurement, 2014).

In a specific case, a vice president of executive development and chief learning officer of a multi-national firm identified five common characteristics that every future leader would possess to be effective in a novel and shifting business and organisational landscape (Peters, 2012):

- Future global leaders demonstrate an extraordinary external focus. The outward focus helps them to increase their perimeter of collaboration and interaction. It is not restricted to customers, rather it encompasses a wide range of stakeholders such as governments, regulators, non-governmental organisations and community groups.

- Adaptation and being Agile are important traits of a leader. Leaders are not only decision makers, they are clear thinkers that link strategy to purpose in a manner that promotes commitment.
- Leaders are creative, as they can imagine and innovate. They are brave enough to take risk and achieve set goals.
- Leaders build great teams. Leaders have the capability to embrace every member, as that is the mantra for strong team building.
- Leaders never rest. Leaders believe in learning endlessly and sharpening their skills and abilities. In addition, they are influencers, as they motivate others to adopt the same route.

4.3 TRAITS OF HIGH POTENTIAL EMPLOYEES

HiPo employees are characterised by extraordinary performance. HiPos are believed to delight their peer employees in the manner that HiPos master skills and deliver results. HiPo employees possess an intrinsic motivation to learn on the job and deliver on outputs. According to the article 'Are you a High Potential?', HiPo individuals possess X factors that differentiate them from other employees in the organisation (Ready, Conger, & Hill, 2010). These four X factors that set HiPo individuals apart are:

X Factor 1 – Drive to Excel: HiPo employees deliver extraordinary performance by going the extra mile. They may become obsessed with delivering extraordinary results, and most of the time these individuals choose work over other things in their personal lives. HiPos value work and life, but the inherent desire to succeed and outperform peers leads them make choices that are perceived as too hard to pursue for a traditional employee (Ready et al., 2010).

X Factor 2 – Catalytic Learning Capability: Continuous learning is important for any employee to achieve sustainable growth. For HiPo individuals, continuous learning transforms itself to action learning capabilities. This inherent cognitive skill allows the HiPos to scan new ideas and absorb them. Furthermore, the HiPo takes learning to another level with immediate experimentation by absorbing the lived experience in learning something new. Regardless of the results, the person learns, adjusts and begins anew (Ready et al., 2010).

X Factor 3 – An Enterprising Spirit: HiPos love challenges and prefer to go out of their comfort zones and indulge in tasks that are complex, involve risk and require critical thinking. Challenges drive these individuals to learn new skills and succeed in their jobs as a vehicle for personal and job satisfaction (Ready et al., 2010).

X Factor 4 – Dynamic Sensors: Since HiPo individuals demonstrate a high-level enthusiasm to pursue any task, they may sometimes lead to wrong decision-making and may get derailed from their career path. In order to overcome this risk, HiPo employees are equipped with dynamic sensors, which help them evaluate the right time and right opportunity by analysing the situation prior to making a quick decision. They are aware of every situation that they need to get into or time to get out of it (Ready et al., 2010).

4.4 HIGH POTENTIALS IN LEAN AND SIX SIGMA

Since HiPo employees are in high demand, an organisation embarking or managing a Lean Six Sigma (LSS) program needs to have a pathway to success for HiPos. At the outset, an organisation should have entry-level positions, such as Yellow Belts (YBs) and Green Belts (GBs) and select candidates who start the LSS journey cautiously. LSS projects are complex, even projects that are scoped for initial LSS candidates, such as GB and perhaps YBs, must go out of their way to perform and deliver results. GB projects typically reside within a candidate's area of professional work or expertise. However, GBs often perform an LSS project while still carrying on their functional duties, which creates competing commitments (Laux, Johnson, & Cada, 2015). The additional LSS tasks for GBs create an opportunity for management to identify those personnel who have HiPo and already reside within an organisation. Challenges go beyond identifying a pool of HiPos though. In reality, HiPos exists in every profession; therefore, the major challenge lies in identifying and retaining these personnel. In the field of LSS, the focus should be towards identifying potential star performers and then developing them to meet their highest potential. Thus, human resource management of LSS talent need not come within the field of Lean or Six Sigma, but in emerging areas of corporate interests.

While Agile as a discipline is inspired and founded upon Lean principles, the adoption of Agile in an LSS strategy provides strategic benefits, including talent management. In the Agile philosophy, the entire process is broken down into achievable small processes to ensure completion of a project. Agile was a concept introduced by the software developers, but now it has been adopted by the organisations to improve process efficiency. The Agile philosophy helps to prioritise work (tasks) and ensures timely completion. Management can develop a HiPo program using the Agile methodology to develop top talent. While Agile is usually applied to software development, Agile is connected to Lean approaches (McNair & Mass, 2010). Agile provides approaches to changing requirements, highlighting individuals over tools, requires collaboration and responds to change (McNair & Mass, 2010). Adoption of an Agile strategy should lead an organisation to designing criterion for selecting the top candidates to take on key roles as LSS practitioners and working with outside functions to become effective strategic leaders (Martin, 2015). LSS leadership, such as Champions and other senior management, play an important role in making decisions regarding projects. This focus should also extend to individuals based upon the Agile tenant of personnel importance, in order to design an effective programme for top talent. With focus on proactive coaching for developing HiPos, organisational leadership can help draw up an outline of a required HiPo candidate.

4.5 DEVELOPING AN AGILE PROGRAM FOR LEAN SIX SIGMA HIPO SELECTION

Employee engagement is one of the most crucial organisational responsibilities. If we concentrate on and determine the reasons why employees switch organisations, the answers likely include that that person does not feel engaged. Employee engagement refers to making the employee feel the value of his/her job. 'Value' is an abstract concept, measuring value is in fact challenging, and varies among individuals. When it comes to HiPos, value remains consistent in describing these individuals. HiPos value work that helps them to learn new skills and drives them to deliver exceptional results. The Agile focus is to develop a HiPo program for identification, selection and retention while fostering the skills required by an individual to fulfil the organisation's strategy, ever evolving, through their LSS strategy.

In the realm of LSS, change is continuous and demands the LSS professional to deliver results in terms of individual performance and productivity. In order to survive the dynamic effects of any organisational process, a practitioner may need to adopt HiPo characteristics. Identifying HiPos for LSS training is measurable. However, developing HiPos using Agile practices requires mindful thinking to identify individuals. Before designing a selection strategy for LSS practitioners, it is important to understand the various roles of these professionals. LSS roles are defined as shown in Fig. 4.1 (Antony et al., 2018; Sunder, 2013).

4.6 LSS HIPO SELECTION PROCESS

Adopting a HiPo selection process is one of the most crucial steps for an organisation developing LSS talent. Selecting the top candidate is always a difficult task and clarity in the selection process is an important principle, so managers can distinguish between a performer and a HiPo. The following five steps are proposed to select HiPos.

Selecting Top Talent for Execution of Projects

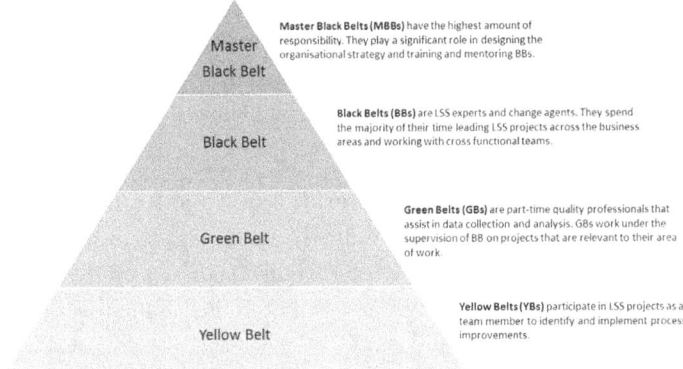

Fig. 4.1. Levels in Lean Six Sigma.

1. **Define performance metrics:** Defining the key organisational metrics helps to evaluate the performance of the candidates. This also enables BBs to provide relevant feedback on their performance. One of the important metrics for LSS project success is critical thinking, which should be closely evaluated. In addition, there must be a focus on evaluating the four X factors that a HiPo possesses: drive to excel, catalytic learning capabilities, enterprising spirit and dynamic sensors.

2. **Conduct a workshop on LSS:** Conducting a workshop on LSS is important as many individuals in the organisation may not have been exposed to the LSS concept. The workshop will allow them to learn about the LSS methodology and use these principles when engaged in an LSS project or in their everyday work.

3. **Identify the individuals who demonstrate interest in LSS:** Every participant in the workshop will not find LSS interesting. Surveys, focus groups, discussions, etc. may be conducted to capture the personal data regarding participants' interest and their willingness to participate in LSS projects.

4. **Invite interested individuals to participate in an LSS project under the supervision of a BB:** It is important to place the interested individuals in a short-term project so that they gain experience in the application of LSS to solve real-world

problems, either as team members or part-time project managers of GB efforts, depending upon the educational pathway of LSS development in the organisation. The important part is to build competence and confidence among individuals in ever-increasing LSS efforts.

5. **Monitor performance and provide continuous feedback:** Monitoring the performance and providing relevant feedback improves the performance of the individuals as it leads to learning by doing. Continuous monitoring also improves the performance of the project.

Based on performance as a team member, star performers may be identified. Continue to engage the star performers in LSS projects. This will enable the MBBs and BBs to identify the HiPo as these star performers are HiPos who can be further trained in LSS and lead to future projects.

4.7 DEVELOPING AN AGILE PROGRAM FOR HIPO IN LSS

The HiPos identified in the previous step can be potential BBs and MBBs for the future. These individuals possess an intrinsic motivation to learn the LSS tools and techniques and use them for process improvement and personal investment. An Agile program for developing the HiPos for future BB and MBB roles is essential for retaining them in the organisation: HiPos could become easily bored with the repetitive or non-challenging tasks. Exposing HiPos to challenging real-world problems, as defined by LSS, can be one of the best ways to retain them.

Critical thinking is a unique attribute of a HiPo. The challenges presented through LSS projects should provide HiPos sufficient opportunity to exercise their critical thinking to solve process-related issues using LSS. When developing a HiPo program, the following eight steps could be considered:

1. **Set customer-centric Agile goals.** The customer is the central to LSS; therefore, all process improvement carried out using LSS principles is to fulfil customer expectations. The idea here is to

set goals for HiPos that are customer centric and Agile. Agile goals focus on quick wins. Quick wins act as a catalyst for HiPos and motivate them to perform better with every project. Successful achievement of these goals is beneficial to the customer as well, as they result in meeting or exceeding customer expectations.

2. **Focus on skill-based learning.** HiPos enjoy learning new things on the job, and process improvement is not restricted to just one set of skills. Performance improvement can vary with every problem as each project is different. While the body of knowledge of tools are not used in a singular project, LSS offers a wide range of techniques that HiPos can learn over time.

    Based on quantitative reasoning, there is a wide range of technology to learn and deploy that are deployed in LSS projects. Training HiPos to use software such as R, Minitab, SPSS, Python or other novel technology can be a value addition to an individual's profile, outlasting project efforts. The use and understanding of statistics HiPos learn helps develop the critical thinking for future BB and MBB profiles.

3. **Provide continuous monitoring and feedback.** When working on an Agile project, it is important for a supervisor to monitor the performance of employees and share frequent feedback, however, formal or informal. For example, a 360-degree feedback is a method to evaluate individual performance. This is an all-round evaluation involving all parties associated with the project to evaluate the performance of the HiPo. However, this method provides feedback typically only once a year: formal and not Agile. Fig. 4.2 illustrates the 360-degree feedback.

    Monthly project reviews and/or phase-gate reviews, paired with the 360-degree feedback, is more timely. A monthly, or more frequent review enables BBs and GBs to meet with their supervisor to discuss how a project is progressing and identify of potential hurdles to overcome. Many organisations use a phase-gate approach that follows the Define–Measure–Analyse–Improve–Control (DMAIC) methodology. Prior to completing a phase and moving on to the next phase, the LSS team leader, which is the BB or GB, meets with the MBB to review progress.

Fig. 4.2. 360-Degree Feedback Mechanism.

The results and key findings of the previous phase may be presented, along with an action plan to complete the next phase as shown in Fig. 4.3. Due to the length of time required to complete BB projects, which is typically six months, many organisations are opting for both monthly project reviews and phase reviews to ensure sufficient and timely monitoring and feedback.

4. **Recognise and reward.** Recognising and rewarding performance enhances the motivation and engagement within the organisation. While HiPos are intrinsically motivated, recognition and rewards may act as a catalyst by recognising their contribution and importance within the organisation. HiPos may also view this as an event to evaluate themselves on the career path and plan their future course of action to reach a desired leadership position.

Fig. 4.3. Phase-gate Monitoring.

5. **Track progress using Agile tools.** HiPos possess X factors, which set them apart. Using Agile tools, HiPos can track their progress constantly, and this may be perceived by HiPos as a driver for X factor development.

6. **Sprint burndown.** Agile emphasises breaking the entire project into small sub-projects known as sprints. This helps the process owners set the goals to be achieved during each sprint and track its progress. A sprint burndown report is used to track the progress of a set goal for a sprint with respect to time. It keeps the team updated on the amount of work that needs to be completed to achieve the set goal for a sprint. Using a sprint burnout in LSS is valuable as process owners and HiPos can track progress in real time to make sure that project stays on track.

7. **Track velocity.** Velocity is a measure of progress made by a project team. Tracking velocity helps to track the backlog of work in each sprint. This helps the team identify the difference between actual and desired output. This metric can be used during the Analyse phase of the DMAIC project to analyse performance gap(s) and identify the root causes that lead to gap reduction.

8. **Chart cumulative flow.** A cumulative flow chart tool may also be used in the Control phase as this technique helps an individual determine if project progress through process improvement is consistent across all affected processes. If the progress is consistent, the flow should be smooth. The chart will also identify any gaps that require attention.

4.8 CAREER PROGRESSION AND LEADERSHIP POSITIONS

Developing HiPos within the organisation will help fill future leadership positions. The star performer identified can be trained to become a GB. Further, with proper training and development they can progress to BB and then MBB. Later, they can also acquire senior leadership positions within the organisations such as Vice

President or Senior Vice President. The advantage of this in-house development program is that it lays the foundation for a strong organisational culture that focuses on continuous improvement. The progression up the career ladder enables individuals to make the right decisions for the organisation and the customer.

What do industry experts have to say on hiring and retaining top talent? Several top industry executives with extensive Lean Six Sigma experience were interviewed. These firms are in heavy manufacturing and embarked on their LSS journey in 2001.

In a Fortune 100 company that is the world's largest construction equipment manufacturer, one of our interviewees spent the bulk of his career in the firm. Currently a Technical Manager, our LSS professional worked broadly across the company and progressed through the ranks, collecting a BB and MBB along the way. He has been involved with developing talent for the company. Our company expert notes that the company has a formal HiPo program. The HiPo program is based upon identification, selection and giving individuals challenging assignments to further develop those skills that individuals need. There is interaction between the HiPo program that the company operates and LSS. The talent flows in both directions as BBs who successfully complete projects are tapped as a HiPo and individuals in the HiPo program are a pool of talent for selection in the LSS ranks. The key is for the individual to be open to new experiences, embrace the challenge and continue to develop as a professional.

A President of a small and medium enterprise (SME) that operates in the US Midwest was interviewed as well. It is a service and manufacturer over a wide range of electrical supplies, including industrial component manufacturing, across the US states of Indiana, Illinois and Ohio. The executive championed LSS at this firm, since the company adopted the strategy in 2001. In that time, LSS has been widely adopted and applied throughout the business. This executive was asked about top talent and LSS. In contrast to the discussions with the Fortune 100 company, the SME offers a different, less formal approach to developing HiPo individuals. The LSS program provides opportunities for the SME to develop HiPo talent. With fewer resources on hand, individuals working as SMEs often have to task switch among roles to get the job done. The ability to adapt, apply creative thinking and a regular mechanism for feedback on the quality of work is important to this SME. LSS offers a path for those individuals to develop into a HiPo and, more importantly, retain the employees. As an SME, with a flat hierarchical organisational structure, the firm works across the enterprise in a lateral fashion to develop top talent.

What does it take to identify such individuals as HiPo? The experts interviewed stressed open mindedness and an attitude for continual change. In a fast-paced job environment, the ability to work in an Agile fashion is an ingredient, based upon frequent customer demand changes. The experts also stressed that talent is developed in a variety of ways. Traditional professional expertise has been a pathway for LSS practitioners, as experts stress that higher education is an important facet in identifying a HiPo pool (Sunder & Mahalingam, 2018). While identifying current personnel for recruitment into LSS, both the Fortune 100 company and the SME firm identify and acquire talent based, in part, on the recruitment of college graduates into their respective firms and shaping the individual into the organisational culture.

The LSS philosophy is deeply encoded at both the above discussed organisations. While both operate with different organisational resources, the quality of products and services are crucial to both. Thus, LSS will continue to play a role in these companies. Their employees, new or current, will continue to undergo a variety of challenges that test their ability to problem solve, demonstrate the capability to adapt, take on new assignments and move out of personal comfort zones. This is what LSS offers top talent, such as HiPo individuals.

5

LEADERSHIP FOR LEAN SIX SIGMA DEPLOYMENT

5.1 INTRODUCTION

Although the importance of LSS in any business setting has been recognised and understood despite its size and nature, the role of leadership for introducing, developing and sustaining LSS as a business process improvement strategy has been a constant battle over the years. Juran et al. (1995) stated that 'attaining leadership for quality requires that senior managers personally take charge of the quality initiative'. The best example for this is explicitly demonstrated by the former CEO of Motorola, Robert Galvin, who has made a habit of making quality the very first item on the agenda of executive staff meetings (Antony, 2015). Several studies have shown that tools and techniques contribute only 20% towards business transformation using any continuous improvement methodologies such as Lean, Six Sigma or even LSS (Mann, 2014; Wilson, 2015; Wincel & Kull, 2013). The remaining 80% necessitates changing the leaders' behaviours and practices and subsequently their thinking.

Research shows an inextricable link between leadership and commitment (Waldman et al., 1998) as the basis of the success of any quality improvement programme such as LSS. Our experience with many organisations suggests that unwavering commitment from top management and business leaders is fundamental for embedding LSS into the organisation's culture, allowing it to overcome the initial scepticism of employees. Leadership has been recognised as a mechanism for embedding cultural values and norms into an organisation. The idea of culture affecting the type of leadership in an organisation has been advanced (Bass, 1990), suggesting the existence of a reciprocal relationship between leadership and culture in organisations (Laureani & Antony, 2018).

Lean Six Sigma has been extremely successful in some organisations, where it is no longer only a cost reduction initiative but has also been embedded into the organisation's way of doing things (well-known examples are Toyota for its renowned production system and GE for Six Sigma). However, many other organisations struggle to turn Lean Six Sigma into a success because of different failure factors (Albliwi, Antony, Halim Lim, & van der Wiele, 2014), and it should be questioned whether different styles and traits of leadership can have an impact on whether the deployment of Lean Six Sigma results in organisational success.

A recent empirical study has shown that leadership is one of the most critical success factors (CSFs) for the successful deployment of LSS (Laureani & Antony, 2018). In this study, 19 CSFs derived from the existing literature were tested in the form of a survey and all participants were asked to rank the CSFs. Over 120 responses from experts in the field of LSS were received which included many LSS Master Black Belts, LSS Black Belts and LSS project champions. Moreover, the following observations were made from the above study:

- Lean Six Sigma transformation is a journey that does not happen overnight; successful leaders are those that can see beyond the difficulties and inspire employees to keep going.

- Successful leadership is able to see the link between Lean Six Sigma and the overall business strategy and its customers as well as communicate this to employees in a clear and compelling vision.

- Successful leadership is able to establish an organisational culture that accelerates Lean Six Sigma implementation.

- Although it is rather typical of organisations that the most experienced professionals are in positions of leadership, this study highlights the importance of involving the top talent in the organisation in Lean Six Sigma, providing them with the right project management tools and making them financially accountable for the success of continuous improvement initiatives such as LSS.

- It is necessary to keep the Lean Six Sigma efforts linked to the financial results of the organisation, making leaders accountable for the financial impacts of their initiatives.

5.2 STRATEGIC SIGNIFICANCE OF LSS LEADERSHIP

Leadership is a collection of behaviours that enables an individual or group of individuals to continually act with more confidence in the face of uncertainty and threat in order to create a desired future. In fact, leadership is about bringing positive change to any organisation. In a real sense, LSS is a change leadership development programme that develops an organisation's leadership capability while at the same time improving quality, reducing operational costs and sustaining competitive advantage.

No leadership development will succeed unless it is recognised and wholeheartedly supported by senior executives. Lean Six Sigma is a leadership development tool because it provides leaders with strategy, methods and tools to improve processes, thereby changing their organisations (Antony & Snee, 2010). Alefari, Salonitis, and Xu (2017) and Angelis, Conti, Cooper, and Gill (2011) suggest that there is a causal link between the leadership actions necessary to transform Lean and the over-arching transformational change.

5.3 ESSENTIAL LEADERSHIP SKILLS FOR SUCCESSFUL DEPLOYMENT OF LSS

The following leadership skills are required for the successful introduction and deployment of LSS in any organisation (Antony & Snee, 2010):

- **Understand how the business works (business acumen):** The first skill requires a change in attitude and focus. Leaders in an LSS environment must understand how the business functions – end to end – to create value for customers. They must understand the key performance measures, gaps between the current and desired performance and financial stakes involved.

- **Knowledge of strategic planning and deployment:** LSS is a strategic approach to business process improvement and hence a sound knowledge of strategic planning and deployment is highly desirable to effectively lead the initiative.

- **Communication:** Effective deployment of LSS requires getting support from key stakeholders and clear, concise and continuous communication with the organisation.

- **Encourages structured and systematic approach to process improvement:** A leader's ability to change processes is greatly enhanced when he or she can use a systematic and structured approach to process improvement. In the past, problem-solving methods were typically informal and not documented. This approach worked well because a small group (two to three people) was usually involved and informal communication was enough. A process improvement methodology such as LSS is different in the sense that the team is usually larger – four to six members work best, but as many as 10 or 12 are sometimes involved (Snee, Kelleher, & Reynard, 1998). Informal problem-solving and improvement methods no longer work in this situation. A common language, roadmap, tools, and sequence and linkage of tools help the team function as a unit with a common thought process.

- **Deals effectively with teams and group dynamics:** Leadership requires working with people in a variety of settings. The ability to recognise when groups of people are interacting effectively or ineffectively is a critical skill. Leaders providing positive feedback when appropriate and intervening and redirecting the group when needed are essential to enabling groups to produce useful results in a timely manner.

- **Plans and manages projects:** Using structured methods, leadership helps team members know where the team stands in the project, where the team is going and what steps and activities the team will conduct to successfully complete the project. 'Making it up as we go along' doesn't work in a team environment.

- **Understands human behaviour:** Leadership requires dealing with people, which in turn requires understanding human behaviour to be effective. The authors dedicate a separate section on leadership behaviour in the next part of the chapter.

5.4 LEADERSHIP BEHAVIOURS FOR LSS TRANSFORMATION

The literature (Mann, 2014; Nogueira, Sousa, & Moreira, 2018) proposes both 'transformation' and 'transactional' leadership behaviours are required. The former concentrates on the efficiency aspects, whilst the latter concentrates upon traits necessary to become facilitators and motivators. Toyota utilises a methodology which involves consistent detection and methodical advancement of its leaders, although this process is not formalised and is not aligned to key values (Liker & Convis, 2012).

Wilson (2015) states a definite requirement exists to have followers, and this is imperative for a leader committed to the LSS initiative. To achieve this, the leaders must be situational leaders and should be able to lead through:

- Character
- Competence and
- Personality

However, to achieve this there are certain characteristics which need to be in place; namely:

- Lean Six Sigma leaders must have a vision with a clear plan to achieve the stated objectives
- The ability to articulate this plan so that followers comprehend it and are prepared to believe and follow it

- The ability to act on the plan despite any obstacles or resistance encountered

Van Assen (2018) advocates varied leadership behaviours for Lean at different hierarchical stages which reinforces the findings of Mann (2009). The leadership behaviours of lower-level managers require greater people-oriented skills to inspire contribution and teamwork whilst integrating greater responsibility. Senior managers need to pursue the vision, improve capabilities and address the performance management aspects. Van Assan (2018) summarises 10 actions and behaviours felt to apply with respect to Lean leadership. These include:

1. The commitment and role modelling necessary
2. Vision towards the true north
3. Empowering employees
4. Fostering a culture of trust
5. Demonstrating respect
6. Coaching and teamwork facilitation
7. Effective target setting
8. Information sharing arrangements and feedback loops
9. Management by facts
10. Celebrating success

5.5 LEADERSHIP CHARACTERISTICS FOR LEAN SIX SIGMA

This section is based on a research study in the form of semi-structured interviews to understand the leadership characteristics for the successful deployment of LSS. A total of 21 experts (LSS Master Black Belts, BBs and Senior Managers) from both service and manufacturing companies were involved in this project (Laureani & Antony, 2017). Lean Six Sigma is a transformational journey for an organisation, radically changing the way things are done. It is necessary for the leader to be visible at the forefront of this journey, personally leading the charge and being identified with it. It is not only the top executive leaders: ensuring top-performing people in all business units and geographies are engaged in the programme which is key to achieving visibility. The following comment points to the idea of senior management constantly reiterating the importance of improvement initiatives: 'There is no substitute for visible leadership by the CEO. And what I mean by that is even if the senior executive cannot meet with individual employees regularly, they should be talking about the initiative virtually every time they give a speech or address employees or write a letter to the shareholders in the annual report. They should be communicating about this personally on a regular basis' – MBB from a large automotive manufacturing company.

Establishing and utilising effective communication systems and structures was deemed good practice in engaging the workforce and achieving buy-in to improve processes. Participants' comments suggested a need for both verbal and visual communication systems as mutually re-enforcing mechanisms for communicating the message. Participants also highlighted the need for leadership to be inspirational: the start of a Lean Six Sigma journey can be worrisome for employees, who may be afraid of potentially losing their job as a result, so it is important for leaders to inspire employees with a compelling vision for the future of the organisation, making it clear what the benefits will be for them.

The importance of the three Rs (Roles, Responsibilities, and Relations) in the context of good leadership practice cannot be overstated. Leaders need to clearly define roles and responsibilities at senior, middle and junior management levels, ensuring anyone involved understands the expectations in rolling out and sustaining the Lean Six Sigma initiative. The roles and responsibilities of good leaders to sustain LSS initiative include:

- Setting strategic direction and goals for the journey clearly indicating the key milestones and the performance indicators at every key stage of the journey.

- Defining and communicating the strategy at all levels adopted by the organisation and create a sense of urgency.
- Empowering employees and making them accountable for improvement of their own processes.
- Creating an environment that promotes creativity, innovation and continual improvement both vertically and horizontally across the organisation.
- Inspiring, motivating, recognising and rewarding employees' contribution at both individual and team levels for process improvement projects.

No matter how successful a Lean Six Sigma initiative appears to be, inevitably there will be operational issues, budget constraints and urgent issues that will divert the organisation's attention from the initiative. It is important that leaders show consistency, an unresolved commitment to the initiative, a strong passion to keep it going and not having it fade in favour of other priorities.

As with any change management initiative, Lean Six Sigma is going to face resistance; not all employees, managers and non-managers, are going to be accepting of changes. It is important that leaders recognise this, identify the areas of greatest resistance and get personally involved to overcome them. Leadership needs to target to the areas of critical resistance, with leaders spending more time in the areas where more resistance is expected.

It is important for leadership to perceive Lean Six Sigma not just as a toolkit for fixing problems, but as a philosophy, a way of thinking, to be ingrained into the workplace culture. Until Lean Six Sigma is referred to as a 'cultural change initiative' in an organisation, it is likely it hasn't been embedded yet and is still in danger of disappearing. A truly successful deployment is one where employees don't refer to Lean Six Sigma as a 'programme' anymore, but it is simply the way things are done. To achieve this, leadership needs to engage with the Lean Six Sigma initiative from the outset, understand the key principles and the potential applications for Lean Six Sigma in alignment with wider organisational strategies and goals, all whilst leading by example, particularly ensuring a transparent and data-driven decision-making process.

Leadership needs to be flexible, adapting to the different stages of maturity. The ability to build trust with colleagues is another essential leadership characteristic; the capacity of building employees' confidence in the approach and competence of leadership itself, with what can be termed as the three Cs model of trust-building for leadership: Connection, Competence and Character. Steven Covey, a renowned leadership authority once said, 'Character is what we are; competence is what we can do. The reality is that character and competence drive everything else in the organization' (Covey, Merrill, & Merrill, 1997). Successful companies are great at developing their workers/employees in both character and competency. If you have competence and character in place but still aren't making progress, you are likely missing the mark when it comes to connection. It is important to bear in mind that connection must be a two-way dialogue and takes continual effort. It is good practice to listen twice as much as you talk. Do this in conjunction with character and competence, and you will build trusting relationships with employees, customers, suppliers and key stakeholders of the business.

5.6 LEADERSHIP STYLES FOR LEAN SIX SIGMA

Lean Six Sigma has been very successful in some organisations, where it is no longer only a cost reduction initiative but has also been embedded into the organisation's way of doing things: more well-known examples are probably GE for Six Sigma (Eckes, 2003). However, many other organisations have been and are struggling to turn Lean Six Sigma into a success, due to different failure factors (Albliwi et al., 2014). Given that leadership has been identified as a CSF, we now turn to investigate specifically which leadership style is more conducive to a successful implementation of Lean Six Sigma in organisations. Of course, many LSS MBBs and BBs play leadership roles in Lean Six Sigma deployment. Lean Six Sigma provides great opportunities for MBBs and BBs to lead business process improvement initiatives in any organisational setting. This section focuses on the style of leadership to implement and sustain the initiative.

A research project was carried out in the form of focus groups at five manufacturing and service companies (three LSS MBBs and two LSS BBs) to determine whether a transformational or transactional style of leadership was being used to deploy Six Sigma (Antony & Snee, 2010). Transactional leadership refers to the contingent exchange between a leader and his or her followers. This implies that followers agree to comply with a leader and deliver the expected effort. Transformational leaders focus on the long-term strategic goals of the business and actively encourage a new look at old methods, stimulates creativity and encourages others to look at problems and issues in a new way. Transactional leaders closely resemble the traditional definition of a manager. Transactional leaders focus on short-term day-to-day leadership issues, encourage followers to set goals and promise rewards for desired performance (Yukl, 2006).

Leaders lead change; process improvement involves change; hence, MBBs and BBs need to act and function as leaders of change. They must provide direction, communicate the purpose, value and progress of the new direction, enable others through training and mentor to implement the new direction, and, finally, recognise and reinforce successful improvements. If Lean Six Sigma is the chosen method of business process improvement strategy for an organisation to sustain the bottom-line results of Lean Six Sigma projects over time, our findings suggest that a transformational leadership style is necessary. The use of transformational leadership by all the Six Sigma professionals interviewed is not surprising when you consider that transactional leadership is similar to the leadership provided by those managers who report to them. The following roles have been found common across all the participants of the interview:

- Coaching and counselling project teams
- Supporting the efforts of the LSS project champion, deployment champion and senior management team
- Delivering results
- Developing and delivering Six Sigma training
- Promoting Six Sigma in the organisation

5.7 SUMMARY

As Lean Six Sigma is one of the most frequently used frameworks for continuous improvement, many organisations have attempted to deploy it with mixed success. Although the literature focuses on the tools and methodologies that underpin Lean Six Sigma, the purpose of this chapter was to highlight leadership's role as a CSF for its deployment and illustrate the specific leadership skills and styles a leader needs to display to increase the chances of a successful deployment.

6

EFFECTIVE TRAINING AND DESIGN OF CURRICULUM FOR DIFFERENT LSS ROLES

6.1 INTRODUCTION

While the Lean Six Sigma (LSS) methodology is experiencing widespread adoption among a variety of businesses and industries, there is an inherent drawback of its misapplication if adequately trained personnel with the proper background are not available. Without well-structured training, planning using the LSS methodology remains misguided. Good training can be accomplished by designing curricula that expose learners to essential concepts and methodologies (Mitra, 2004).

Organisations are a conglomerate of staff from different backgrounds and employees may not be aware of the LSS methodology. This becomes more apparent in organisations embarking on the LSS journey for the first time or are in nascent stages of startup. Hence, it is necessary to impart training to all the stakeholders; champions, Master Black Belts (MBBs), Black Belts (BBs), Green Belts (GBs), other operational support staff including Yellow Belts (YBs), and others who are involved in LSS implementation, as each of these stakeholders have specific roles to play in the LSS journey. Training duration and curriculum for each role must be carefully planned.

Champion training. Champions need to select good projects, select the right people for LSS, and monitor the progress of the overall LSS implementation status. Further, it is necessary to plan the training for champions in order to select the appropriate projects, select individuals for BB and GB training and monitor the progress of projects. This training can be designed for a duration of one to two days based on the LSS maturity of the organisation. Champion training predominantly covers leadership aspects, change management and strategic elements of LSS rather than providing a technical toolkit. Champions should also be well versed on handling resistance to change, change acceleration process, importance of metrics in business, selection and prioritising right projects for improvements, data-orientation, analytical thinking and decision-making, and creative and structured problem-solving.

MBB training. Champions and Master Black Belts (MBB) training should overlap but typically are not identical. MBBs need strong technical orientation and people skills. However, MBBs need little business orientation, unlike champions who need strong business orientation and less people orientation with no need for any technical orientation (George, 2003). MBBs are experienced Black Belts (BBs) that have exceeded at project execution and led LSS projects for a few years. LSS project experience is necessary to move forward to the role of MBB, which is a full-time practitioner and facilitator in LSS that mentor GBs and BBs (Ingle & Roe, 2001). According to ASQ (formerly the American Society for Quality) (2019), MBBs have outstanding leadership ability, are innovative and demonstrate a strong commitment to the practice and advancement of quality and improvement in organisations.

BB training. BBs are considered leaders of the LSS projects and the overall responsibility of LSS project management. BBs are expected to be change agents with teaching, mentoring and cross-functional stakeholder management skills. BBs also possess a high degree of technical mastery of the LSS tools. BB training typically is conducted over a four-month period. A week of training is conducted each month, and the remaining three weeks during each month provides time to apply the concepts to a real-world project. BB training should include various technical aspects of LSS and advanced statistical tools. Most organisations certify BBs not merely by attending the training programs but through the demonstration of learning by applying the concepts in a project (Ingle & Roe, 2001). For example, BBs in General Electric are certified after completing two to five financially successful projects. Other organisations (e.g. Motorola, DuPont and Microsoft) test the capabilities of BBs through a written test alongside demonstration of successful project management (Marx, 2008).

GB training. Green Belts (GBs) are expected to have intermediary LSS technical knowledge for successful implementation of medium sized functional projects. GBs are generally considered part-time quality professionals, unlike BBs who typically work on cross-functional projects as full-time quality professionals. Hence, the GB training includes intermediary level LSS tools and various techniques for data collection and analysis.

YB training. Yellow Belts (YBs) are expected to apply the basic tools of LSS in a business process improvement project and follow the Define, Measure, Analyze, Improve, and Control (DMAIC) problem-solving methodology. The project focus of YBs can be quite narrow, yet the savings to the bottom line can be generous. The YB training is a low-cost, basic overview typically for front-line employees or team members to understand what exactly the company is trying to achieve using LSS (Setter, 2010).

6.2 LEAN SIX SIGMA CURRICULUM

Several existing research studies have outlined contemporary content for each of the five traditional phases of a LSS initiative, through DMAIC (Cudney, Sandilya, Materla, & Antony, 2019; Hoerl, 2001; Rodgers, Antony, Edgeman, & Cudney, 2019). For example, Hoerl (2001) proposed a curriculum model for BBs that is similar to the body of knowledge outlined by ASQ. One important aspect of the model proposed by Hoerl (2001) is the rationale behind the use of certain tools and the interpretations of the results as opposed to emphasis on theory. Further, the significant contribution of the entire curriculum is the integration of the various tools through a project approach.

Trainers and educators should place each of these interpretations into perspective and stress statistical thinking rather than just a procedural discussion of the statistical tools, which is normally the process found in a majority of the seminars conducted training. Practical thinking is not stable, but rather it is formed and evolves in line with specific practices, contexts and professional requirements. It is necessary to reflect on how LSS can become a relevant tool for improvement, not only of practice but also of the practical knowledge when based on the concerns and teaching philosophy of the different LSS belts. Apart from highlighting the LSS materials used in the teaching and learning process, it is important to focus on the educator's skills as habits, attitudes, knowledge and beliefs (Soto Gómez, Serván Núñez, Pérez Gómez, & Peña Trapero, 2015).

6.3 LSS TEACHING AND TRAINING

Knowing the material and being knowledgeable with the content does not mean that an instructor is a good teacher. Demonstration of affective characteristics should be considered as a measure of a teacher's effectiveness. Trainees and students desire encouraging, enthusiastic and approachable instructors. These techniques require awareness rather than training. Educators should also understand that training has a significant positive effect on job-related behaviours and individual performance. However, not all training is equal. The way the training is designed and delivered has a profound influence on learning, behaviour change, performance and profitability. Many features have been directly associated with improved employee and organisational outcomes, including training needs assessment; purpose, objectives and outcomes; relevant content; active demonstration; opportunities for practice; regular feedback; and post-training environment.

Training needs assessment. It is critical to identify who should attend training, what skills they should develop and what are the ultimate strategic objectives.

Purpose, objectives and outcomes. After conducting a training needs assessment, the purpose, objectives and outcomes should be identified and be communicated to trainees in a clear and easy-to-understand way. Communicating how the training will be applied and what outcomes are expected increases the motivation to learn (Noe, 2008).

Relevant content. Training should include content that is directly linked to trainee job experiences (Noe & Colquitt, 2002). This makes intuitive sense, but when ignored it can reduce the impact of training on performance.

Active learning. Live demonstration of the target skills and processes is essential. Through these demonstrations, trainees understand how to model the desired behaviour, which also enhances learning and engages participants in the training, regardless of the topic (Noe & Colquitt, 2002). Consider personal communications training as an example. The trainer may practice effective active listening skills through a role-play with a willing participant. In an engine repair class in the mechanical engineering field, the trainer might bring an engine and demonstrate how to bore out the cylinder.

Opportunities for practice. Providing trainees with multiple opportunities to practice results in effective training programs for acquiring the skills they have learned during class time. The purpose is to provide a trainee with a safe place to try newly acquired skills. This may be achieved by building application exercises into the training workshops themselves. In these workshops, the trainees can make mistakes without worrying about the consequences or repercussions, which further enables them to learn through failures (Noe & Colquitt, 2002).

Regular feedback. Feedback during training is a crucial component in effective training programs. The feedback can be given during the practice itself or after exercises (Noe & Colquitt, 2002). The feedback should be constructive and directly related to how the trainee performed the task. The feedback should never focus on personal characteristics.

Post-training environment. Research has shown that the post-training environment should offer training opportunities to continue to apply their new skills. If the post-training environment does not support the trainee with opportunities to perform the newly acquired skills, the training will have little to no impact on trainee performance and organisational utility (Arthur, Bennett, Edens, & Bell, 2003).

6.4 COURSE PREPARATION

When individuals understand the foundational principles of LSS and realise their potential, they should a holistic approach to solving problems. The team approach to solving problems, which uses cross-functional team members from a variety of areas, can then be adopted.

The first step in preparing for a LSS course is to determine the course objectives. The choice of textbook/training materials, type and order of assignments, and teaching techniques involved in course planning should derive from course objectives (McKeachie, 1978). The list of training objectives should be outlined by the LSS trainer to develop a course plan. Writing out the course objectives helps to clarify the LSS training flow and appropriate exercises. The objectives should point clearly to how the training may be assessed to determine if the objective has been achieved. The assessment is utilised to further enhance and modify course structure (Svinicki & McKeachie, 2013).

Another critical decision is the type of instruction for a course, which may vary by course objective and topic. For some course goals and topics, a regular lecture presentation may suffice. For other topics, a group discussion may be preferable to provide interaction among trainees. Cooperative learning or role-playing techniques may be also useful to engage trainees. Discussions on the implications of this material, how it applies within their work area, or a case study exercise are common techniques used in LSS instruction.

6.5 SOFT SKILLS TRAINING

LSS professionals are in demand as companies want to reduce their costs and enhance their profit potential. LSS practitioners should have the knowledge to reduce waste and variation to make optimum use of available resources. In addition to their statistical and process knowledge, they should have the essential soft skills to work with cross-functional teams from across the organisation. These skills include positive attitude, leadership skills, communication skills, business process understanding and management skills (Brown, 2015).

Positive attitude. A positive attitude is a must for an efficient LSS practitioner. In addition, they must be a firm believer that they can achieve the tasks and goals of the project. Moreover, LSS practitioners should be a role model for their team members and support motivation among team members. LSS practitioners should provide assistance or training to team members who experience difficulty in understanding certain tools or concepts (Brown, 2015).

Leadership skills. One of the crucial characteristics of a LSS practitioner is leadership skills. LSS practitioners must be able to manage a diverse project team and encourage members to work to their potential (Brown, 2015).

Communication skills. Without clear and consistent communication, objectives cannot be accomplished. LSS practitioners should have excellent communication skills in order to effectively convey information to team members as well as top officials in a clear and understandable manner. In addition to strong oral communication skills, LSS practitioners must also possess good writing and presentation skills to be able to communicate project status, which is shared with team members, MBBs, Champions, as well as other stakeholders (Brown, 2015).

Business process understanding. It is important for LSS practitioners to understand all the aspects of the business process in order to take a systems perspective and deliver results. This will also help them to identify the opportunities for improvement in the business processes, which often crosses multiple business functions, and develop effective action plans that benefit all areas. This systems view enables the LSS practitioner to improve the business process and enabling the team to provide efficient and timely results (Brown, 2015).

Management skills. An LSS practitioner needs to be organised as they must balance time, resources and budgets. During regular reviews with the team and Champion, the LSS practitioner will provide updates on where the project currently is with respect to schedule, budget and resources. If there are any discrepancies in these areas, the LSS practitioner must report the issue and convey information to the appropriate decision-maker, which is often the Champion or stakeholder. By providing timely updates, they can obtain feedback and make necessary adjustments quickly to get the project back on track. In other words, they should be able to manage the project and team in an efficient manner (Brown, 2015).

6.6 CURRICULUM DEVELOPMENT

In order to develop and execute a comprehensive LSS curriculum, senior management must use a systematic approach to the program roll-out. Generally, the curriculum development process involves three phases: planning the curriculum, establishing curriculum content and implementing the curriculum (Finch & Crunkilton, 1999). The decision-making process plays a crucial role in each of these three phases.

The curriculum development process is complex as there are many aspects that are related and dependent on multiple steps. This process involves decision-making from senior leadership, which should be made relative to policies, procedures for prioritisation, program and course selections.

When designing the LSS curriculum for the different LSS professional levels, it is more beneficial to use backward design. The backward curriculum design method places learning outcomes and LSS understanding at the centre of course design and then identifies the methods the instructor can support the LSS trainees. According to Wiggins, and McTighe (2005), 'Teaching is a means to an end. Having a clear goal helps educators to focus our planning and guide purposeful action toward the intended results'. The backward design process proceeds in three steps (Wiggins et al., 2005) as shown in Fig. 6.1.

Step 1. Identify the learning outcomes. First, it is important to articulate the learning outcomes and desired results for the course. In other words, identifying what the organisation needs their LSS practitioners to know and be able to apply. A learning outcome is a statement that describes what knowledge, skills, abilities and/or dispositions the LSS practitioners should acquire as a result of a

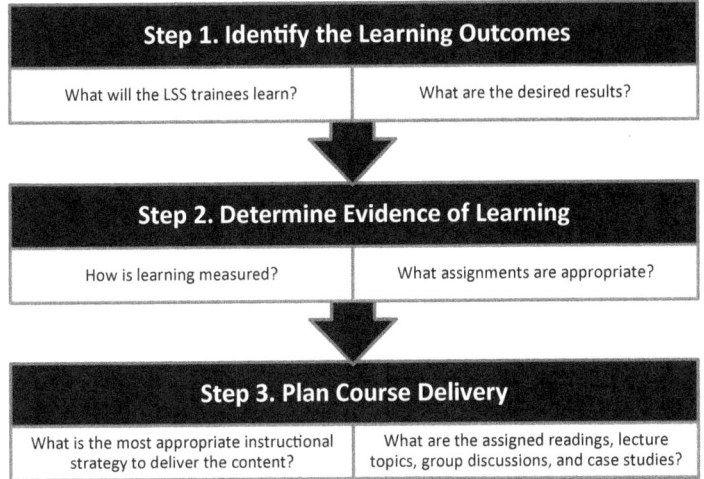

Fig. 6.1. Backward Design Process.

learning experience (or the course as a whole). Learning outcomes are expressed in one of the following schemes:

1. LSS practitioners will be able to......

2. ... action verb

3. ... specific knowledge/ability/disposition that LSS practitioners will achieve.

For example, LSS practitioners will be able to create, identify, evaluate and analyse a value stream map.

In all likelihood, there will be numerous learning outcomes in each course, which will not have an equal emphasis or level of mastery required. Therefore, the MBB and/or trainer will need to prioritise the learning outcomes to determine what is most important. Answering several questions can help prioritise the learning outcomes that are essential, important, and nice to know. Recognising the relative importance of the learning outcomes will help design the course in meaningful, integrated ways (Wiggins et al., 2005).

Highest priority. Which learning outcomes refer to the 'big ideas' in the course? What are facts, concepts, theories and methods that are crucial for LSS practitioners to understand? These are called 'enduring understandings' and are the most essential learning outcomes.

Moderate priority. Which learning outcomes are related to the important knowledge, skills and abilities that LSS practitioners must acquire? These facts, concepts, theories and methods are important building blocks that provide a foundation to support the big ideas of the course and will also prepare LSS practitioners for future learning.

Lower priority. Which learning outcomes relate to the knowledge, skills and abilities that are still necessary but less essential? In other words, while the LSS practitioners might not master these facts, concepts, theories or methods, it may still be valuable to provide them with some exposure to or familiarity with these.

Step 2. Determine Acceptable Evidence. The second step is to focus on the ways to determine what data should be gathered as evidence that LSS trainees are achieving the learning goals of the course. In other words, Step 2 prompts questions such as: What will it look like when trainees 'get it'? What does LSS learning look like? How will the learning outcomes be measured? Consider different types of evidence to measure if the learning outcomes are achieved such as application of LSS tools to an industry project, problem sets, group presentations and group discussions. These evaluation methods help gauge each trainee's achievement of the learning outcomes (Wiggins et al., 2005).

Step 3. Plan course delivery. After identifying and prioritising the learning outcomes and determining the ways to assess learning, the third step is to plan the specific instructional strategies or learning experiences to support the LSS trainees. Instructional strategies for course delivery often include lectures, discussions, experiments, readings, homework assignments and projects. In order to identify the appropriate strategy for content areas, it is useful to answer some important enquiries such as: what is the most appropriate way to deliver the content? What will be the assigned readings, lectures topics, group discussions and case studies to support learning.

Bloom's taxonomy can be used to focus curricula on specific parts of the framework to ensure the LSS trainees demonstrate the proper cognitive abilities before moving on to the next topic. A modified version of Bloom's Taxonomy for course design is provided by Tolman (2001). This approach also provides clear and quantifiable goals for trainees to achieve. Based on the level of skill or knowledge required for each topic, the appropriate learning objectives may be developed using the measurable verbs for each level to elicit the proper types of responses. For example, trainees can be asked to summarise, list or interpret, which will help their basic understanding of the related concept. Further, trainees can be asked to improve, justify or distinguish, which suggest that they are using critical thinking skills.

The training should move from lower to higher levels of learning through course materials, topics, lectures, assignments and in-classroom activities that are fine-tuned to help them succeed. Following the framework of Bloom's taxonomy, assignments and classroom learning can be restructured to ensure that they fall in line with each level in succession and that LSS trainees have the critical thinking tools to lead LSS projects.

It is also important to engage learners through active learning and participation through hands-on exercises. For example, with content that falls in the 'recall' category of Bloom's taxonomy, instead of sitting back and absorbing information, instructors and trainers could ask trainees to challenge each other to recollect facts, or, make a list at the end of class of the most important concepts or facts they learned that day. For topics in the 'apply' category of Bloom's taxonomy, trainers can spark class discussion of problems and comparisons to examine how the topic relates to the learners' job function or industry.

Being explicit about expectations during training also helps guide trainees in the right direction, which is a great application of metacognition within Bloom's taxonomy. For example, the LSS trainer can inform the trainees that they should know the components of an effective LSS business case, why each component is important and how the components work together to achieve the industrial goals of the company by the middle of the define phase. Providing the required expectations and the deadline encourages LSS trainees to take responsibility for their own learning.

The LSS curriculum and education program must prepare learners for the effective usage and implementation of LSS through activity-based projects and problem-based curriculum for different LSS roles. Using a high-quality educational model, combined with an engaged network of professionals and corporate partners, enables LSS learners to develop the skills needed to succeed. The developed curriculum needs to be consistently reviewed and improved by LSS professionals, university educators, and industry experts. The LSS curriculum should align with industry objectives and business. The following are some important features for a proposed curriculum:

- Based on contextual projects and problems
- Integrated with business and industrial needs
- Provide with breadth and depth of content
- Supported by comprehensive professional development for educators
- Sustained and updated through industrial and academic experts.

The high-quality educator professional development model will be applied over the phased approach to fully support LSS educators. The first phase is instructor readiness, which aims to provide educators with knowledge of teaching techniques, effective teaching strategies and teaching tips with the focus on core knowledge/skill. The second stage is core program preparation, which involves in-person training for teacher development activities on the program content. Finally, continuous learning for educators is provided, as needed, with a focus on content knowledge of teaching practice.

6.7 CURRICULUM ASSESSMENT

In developing a curriculum and training for LSS roles, it is important to focus on what needs to be achieved by the learners using Bloom's taxonomy as a guide, rather than focusing on whether a specific activity will contribute toward their overall performance. Concrete learning objectives should be developed for each stage with clear expectations provided to the learner. Actions or expectations for each assignment should be identified along with the appropriate level for application. Then, assessment techniques and questions should be matched to the activity. Training activities should be selected that will enable the expected results (Harlen & James, 1997). Participant learning should be assessed to ensure alignment between content delivery and achievement of learning outcomes using both formative and summative assessment, which are discussed in detail next.

Formative assessment. Formative assessment is an informal check for learner understanding of a topic, which often involves feedback. This feedback may or may not be 'graded'; however, it is a way for educators to gauge how well learners are doing. Further, formative assessment is not a scale that determines the success or failure of a trainee or student. It is used as a continued tool for instruction (Harlen & James, 1997). For example, YBs should have a basic knowledge of LSS. Therefore, the 'Remember' and 'Understand' levels of Bloom's taxonomy are appropriate for many topics to assess learning. For concepts that require critical thinking skills, such as those in the Analyze, Create, and Evaluate levels of Bloom's taxonomy, oral or written work may be appropriate. Assignments may paint a picture of how much the LSS trainees have learned to date so educators can adjust course materials or instructional strategy. This will help better prepare learners to succeed when it comes time for summary assessment.

Summative assessment. Summative assessment is used to evaluate learning at the end of a topic by comparing performance to a standard or benchmark. This typically involves major assessments such as a final project. Bloom's taxonomy is also applicable for assignments and examination toward the LSS certification. Typically, exams cover material and learning of basic or bridging skills such as remember, understand and apply (Harlen & James, 1997). The latter half of the content may be assessed for critical thinking skills such as analyze, create and evaluate. Based on the LSS role, trainees should be able to apply their knowledge to everyday situations beyond course material, provide informed opinions and defend them, considering additional questions that need to be addressed. Summative assessments provide indication of a deeper level of learning that fits within the critical thinking levels of Bloom's taxonomy.

Moreover, the developed curriculum and training designed for all LSS levels should emphasise how to execute the organisation's strategic objectives as well as the key factors that influence the effective and successful execution of the strategic plan. Strategic planning focuses on fundamental decisions and actions that shape and guide the whole organisation's objective and policy. Developing such a strategic plan is the main responsibility of senior leaders; however, it is the responsibility of mid-level leaders to translate this strategy into operational-level plans and actions that result in execution throughout the organisation. Without mid-level leadership buy-in and emphasis, the strategic plan cannot be cascaded throughout the organisation. One of the most important key factors in executing the organisation's strategic plan is culture. Therefore, it is important to highlight the fact that culture is not the enemy of strategy and performance, but an equal player in the game, not to be underestimated or overlooked (Harlen & James, 1997).

6.8 CHALLENGES, LESSON LEARNT AND SUSTAINABILITY

LSS is a powerful business process improvement strategy that has been around for many years. Yet, curriculum development for different LSS roles is still in the early stages. In developing LSS curriculum, management and trainers face a number of challenges as well as some lessons learned.

It is important to be clear and decisive at the beginning with the objectives. Detailed outlines of the topics that will be included in your curriculum should be created in order to guide development. To avoid the problem of including too much at once, teams should properly scope the objectives at the outset. To determine the depth of the content, in addition to the expected applications of the material in your curriculum, the following two questions should be considered: (1) what should the trainee learn? and (2) what should the trainee apply? (Pappa, 2010).

To ensure the effectiveness of the implemented curriculum, trainers should ensure that interaction is included to reinforce the concept. Trainees should be given the opportunity to practice and apply the concepts to their own projects (Pappa, 2010).

A critical part of developing a curriculum is creating a sustainable curriculum that has the seeds of development inside itself. This can be achieved by making use of trainee feedback. Trainees are the best source of information that will help to continuously improve the program. Trainee suggestions or recommendations can be received throughout the training so that feedback is documented and understood. In addition, the curriculum will need occasional review and adjustment to ensure exercises, videos and examples are relevant and timely (Pappa, 2010).

6.9 SUMMARY

It is necessary to provide training to all employees while implementing Lean Six Sigma (LSS) in the organisation. This includes the Champions, MBBs, BBs, GBs and other operational support staff including YBs and White Belts (WBs) as each of these stakeholders has a specific role to play in the LSS journey. To make the best use of time and provide appropriate content coverage, the training duration and curriculum for each of the belts must be carefully planned. For instance, the training course of LSS (WB) White Belt is typically a one-day course that covers an overview of LSS including the importance of the DMAIC methodology, importance of waste analysis, variation reduction in processes, and process flow using value stream mapping. LSS WBs are expected to identify and work on simple and effective continuous improvement projects that provide incremental improvements on their own daily processes. The purpose of this chapter is to provide a detailed explanation on the curriculum in a typical LSS program and what is required to achieve certification through effective training.

7

DEVELOPMENT OF REWARDS AND RECOGNITIONS FOR LSS

7.1 INTRODUCTION

According to Kotter (2008), rewards and recognitions should be an inherent part of any change management initiative to align and boost the motivation of staff and morale of teams in organisations. Lean Six Sigma programs require staff across different organisational levels to exhibit high energy and efforts towards a successful deployment; hence a platform to recognise staff for their efforts in the continuous improvement journey becomes essential. Most importantly, Lean Six Sigma is not merely a one-time effort of executing projects, but a continuous improvement journey. Therefore, keeping staff motivated on a consistent basis is an important factor for its success. In other words, rewards and recognition are one of the critical success factors for Lean Six Sigma. According to a survey-based research study amongst global LSS professionals, it was found that staff involvement in Lean Six Sigma projects by itself is a motivation factor to the employees, and Lean Six Sigma is claimed to be a management strategy to drive higher employee satisfaction in organisations alongside customer satisfaction (Sunder, 2013). In addition, there are several ways in which rewards and recognitions could be organized in firms for a successful Lean Six Sigma deployment. This chapter discusses the importance of rewards and recognitions system, and various associated strategies that a firm could employ during its Lean Six Sigma journey.

7.2 WHY REWARDS AND RECOGNITIONS?

Motivational theory (Maslow, 1943) and the theory of self-determination (Gagné & Deci, 2005) endorsed the importance of rewards and recognitions in organisations. While motivational theorists advocate the need for power, affiliation and sense of achievement in staff, self-determination theory highlights that employees have three psychics needs, i.e. need for competence, autonomy and relatedness. In our practical experience, we have seen two types of people in organisations, especially at front-line and mid-management levels. The first kind are the people who are intrinsically motivated or self-motivated and they seldom need an external stimulus to help them perform in organisations. But the bitter fact is that the proportion of such people is very less, and hence the second type becomes important for focus. The second type of people are those who perform positively when motivation is provided to them. Though scholars may disagree that motivation and performance may not have a linear relationship in organisations, it really doesn't matter for a practitioner whether this relationship graph is a straight line (linear) or a curved line (non-linear) when plotted with motivation in X-axis and employee performance in Y-axis. What really matters is to realise that external means of motivation is a proven and endorsed way of making people perform in firms.

This phenomenon of motivation is an interesting one as it could be both tangible and intangible, termed here as rewards and recognitions, respectively. Both of these play a significant role in keeping up the motivation levels of the staff towards delivering a positive and desired performance. A fundamental difference between rewards and recognitions is that rewards are transactional, and recognitions are relational. In other words, rewards are associated with 'if-then' ways of working. They are conferred in the context that 'if you do "X" only then, you will get "Y" in return'. For example, a manager assigning a project to an employee sets the expectation that if the project is delivered on time as per the customer expectations, then the staff member will be rewarded with a renewal of their job contract. Recognition, on the other hand, is more to do with relational exchange between individuals. For example, the best performer in the team gets a better appraisal score as a recognition towards consistent positive performance in comparison with their peer workers. While rewards may be great for attracting people towards a desired outcome, recognition is considered as a tool for sustaining this attraction for retaining the motivation.

In many cases both rewards and recognitions are interlinked. For example, a staff who gets promoted to next level in the organisational hierarchy as a result of a consistent good performance is both a reward and a recognition. On the other hand, an individual can be recognised without giving a reward. A spontaneous pat on the back or a praise in public, an email of appreciation, a mention of a staff name in a leadership gathering, etc. are recognitions that still contribute to staff motivation without any tangible reward associated with them.

While managers follow different strategies when it comes to rewards and recognitions based on several organisational and individual factors, what really matters in the workplace is helping employees feel appreciated. Thus, rewards and recognitions become important. Especially, in the project management context, which is generally challenging in organisations when compared to managing day-to-day operations, rewards and recognitions become extremely important and, in many cases, mandatory. Many employees who contribute towards the success of projects may not really have any benefit directly attributed to them, and hence rewards and recognitions are critical to keep them contributing for the projects' success. Lean Six Sigma projects, which generally involve changes (rather improvements) from process level to policy level, involve a great amount of change management. It is natural for an employee to expect 'what is in it for me' for changing (a behaviour, process, policy or even a strategy). This is where rewards and recognitions become even more important for creating a culture that embraces change. The next section elaborates in detail specific types of rewards and recognitions that positively effect a Lean Six Sigma program.

7.3 TYPES OF REWARD AND RECOGNITION SYSTEMS EFFECTIVE FOR LSS

Rewards and recognitions act as reinforcement machines to create a continuous improvement culture. While it is important to have measurable goals for desired actions in a Lean Six Sigma project environment, it becomes equally important to reinforce the measurement system by rewarding and recognising people when they achieve the project goals. This generally doesn't happen organically in the initial stages of Lean Six Sigma deployment and is hence essential to be planned and implemented by leaders within the organisation's overall strategic deployment. Top management should provide strategic definitions for various rewards and recognitions and associate them with a defined success of Lean Six Sigma initiatives. This can manifest in many forms that are discussed next. These definitions need to further cascade down the organisational hierarchy for mid-level managers to leverage them in daily activities. In other words, for a successful and long-lasting Lean Six Sigma initiative that eventually builds a culture of continuous improvement in organisations, rewards and recognitions should act as a top-down 'system' where everyone in the firm has a role to play (strategic or operational or tactical).

7.3.1 The Carrot Strategy

The carrot strategy is common in organisations. Here, the principle of positive motivation is used to attract people for engaging and delivering on Lean Six Sigma projects. The engagement of staff at any capacity gets recognised here. Be it an idea for improvement, or a potential interest to lead a Lean Six Sigma project, or a successful delivery of a process improvement effort, everything gets a share of reward or recognition here. We call this a 'carrot' strategy as it doesn't force employees to contribute for Lean Six Sigma, but when they do, they get a carrot (reward or recognition) for its effect. This is recommended for Lean Six Sigma start-ups, i.e. when an organisation is in its nascent stages of Lean Six Sigma deployment where the focus is to draw more employee participation by source and not by force.

7.3.2 The Stick Strategy

Unlike the carrot strategy, this type of rewards and recognition system is based on the principle of negative motivation. This is where the reinforcement of participation in Lean Six Sigma initiatives happen really top-down. We call this the 'stick' strategy as every staff is expected to contribute to Lean Six Sigma in their own capacity. In other words, if someone doesn't contribute to the Lean Six Sigma agenda, they may have to face some kind of penalty in the organisation. This system is not recommended unless there are a few groups of people in the organisations that influence the Lean Six Sigma programs negatively. In the real world, we have seen several political situations in organisations where a few management personnel (with authority and position) resist Lean Six Sigma for several reasons. It may be due to peer-level competition where they feel that supporting Lean Six Sigma, which is a brainchild of their peer-level competitors, may hinder their professional growth, or sometimes they simply resist due to other political reasons. The 'stick' discussed above becomes essential in these kinds of situations (where the carrot strategy doesn't work) to get everyone on the same page towards the success of Lean Six Sigma, not only to realise its return on investment (ROI), but to create a culture of continuous improvement in a long run.

7.3.3 The Carrot Stick Strategy

It is naturally important for managers to balance both positive and negative motivation in the organisational context. The carrot stick strategy, which is a combination of the two types, is an effective strategy for Lean Six Sigma implementations when they mature to a greater level in their deployment journeys (not in early stages). As a firm's maturity of Lean Six Sigma improves, it becomes essential to sustain the resultant culture, and here the carrot stick strategy comes in handy. This is where the Lean Six Sigma agenda gets into individual objectives of staff members at all levels. When someone performs well on these objectives, they get a carrot. Similarly, someone who doesn't meet the Lean Six Sigma objectives gets a stick. Here carrot can be a reward or a recognition, and the stick can be a penalty as per the strategic directions of the top management as discussed above.

7.3.4 The Carrots Competition Strategy

This is a special and focused type of rewards and recognitions system where organisational leaders reinforce a sense of competition amongst the employees to contribute to Lean Six Sigma. This could manifest as an effective reward system at different levels. For example, at an individual level, the best process improvement idea/suggestion contributor or the best LSS project manager gets rewarded. Similarly, a business function that makes the highest contribution to LSS projects gets rewarded at the year end. Here, it is essential for business leaders to promote constructive competition amongst individuals or teams towards achieving the strategic objectives of Lean Six Sigma. In our experience, we found this strategy to be effective when the top management is determined to increase the rate of Lean Six Sigma maturity at a faster pace.

7.3.5 The Spontaneous Carrot Strategy

The carrots competition system makes sense, but it has two drawbacks as an actual motivational method. It occurs as an annual activity, and hence competition becomes a seasonal ceremony, and thus does little to reinforce day-to-day behaviours. Here, it is important to recollect that Lean Six Sigma is not merely doing projects, but a real cultural change can be observed when it reflects in the day-to-day behaviours of employees. Hence, a spontaneous system that promotes competition is more relevant. Here, recognitions are more valid than rewards, as they come to employees as sportive surprises. For example, spot awards, team celebrations, simply communicating the results and impact of good work can help workers have intrinsic motivation by seeing the value of their own efforts. In the long run, this strategy not only helps enable a Lean Six Sigma culture, but also promotes a healthy and ongoing performance management system. However, one problem with this strategy is that it creates one winner, and often many losers. Often the same individual wins the recognition every time, leading many others to feel demotivated.

It is naturally interesting to apply a relevant rewards and recognition strategy in organisations to enable a healthy Lean Six Sigma program that could sustain over a period of time. Every strategy is executable within appropriate contextual applicability, and at the same time has drawbacks. There is no one good or bad strategy among those discussed. Managers should use their cognition to decide which among works well for them. In fact, a combination of these reward and recognition strategies should also be examined for success of Lean Six Sigma.

7.4 REWARDS AND RECOGNITIONS – A MANAGEMENT STRATEGY FOR EFFECTIVE CHANGE MANAGEMENT

Not all forms of rewards and recognitions are created equal, nor are they all successful. In reality, the meaning behind the reward or recognition is more important than the reward and recognition itself. A reward for the sake of it cannot attract staff in the long run, and this will negatively impact the sustainability of Lean Six Sigma. Hence, managers should be mindful of rewards and recognition as a tool for change management rather than a mere ceremony. Here are a few tips to make this happen with focused efforts. First, managers should seek ways to personalise the rewards and recognitions so that each individual employee feels valued. Second, make rewards and recognition everyone's job. Managers need not be the only ones handling rewards, and employees should be encouraged to practice peer-to-peer recognition. Third, rewards and recognitions should be spontaneous as much as possible. Just like feedback, which is powerful when given immediately, rewards and recognitions too are more impactful when they happen spontaneously.

A successful change management strategy should encompass five focused stages, namely awareness, desire, knowledge, ability and reinforcement, commonly referred to as ADKAR.

Awareness: Ensure that employees are aware of the Lean Six Sigma initiative and the associated rewards and recognitions that are defined for the initiative.

Desire: Create desire in employees to participate in the program and win the rewards and recognitions. This should be performed through any of the previously discussed strategies.

Knowledge: Once the employees start participating in the Lean Six Sigma initiative, the knowledge which they gain in the due course should be further leveraged to draw more motivation in them. This is possible when the rewards and recognitions get improved or revised periodically, based on the learnings levels that employees carry, and the maturity of the Lean Six Sigma program.

Ability: The rewards and recognitions should be seen as an approach to change management towards developing an ability of Lean Six Sigma in staff. Making it as a mere ritual carries no practical meaning.

Reinforcement: The actions that demonstrate a healthy rewards and recognition system should be reinforced by a choice of appropriate strategy (see discussion in Section 7.3) and a pattern of repeated behaviour (consistency). Top management should ensure that the rewards and recognitions program is be governed through reinforcement top-down to make it everyone's job.

7.5 CONCLUSIONS

This chapter explained why rewards and recognitions are important and how they can make a positive effect on the Lean Six Sigma journeys in firms. Rewards being tangible and transactional naturally have an immediate influence on the staff. At the same time, a genuine recognition is more powerful though it is intangible and relative. Several strategies that are proposed in this chapter will be handy to practitioners in the field of continuous improvement to handle change management effectively through rewards and recognitions. Though there is no one best strategy to employ, managers are advised to use their contextual cognition to identify a suitable 'rewards and recognition' strategy for their respective Lean Six Sigma programs. This chapter concludes by emphasising that the rewards and recognitions should be an inherent part of every Lean Six Sigma deployment to attract, develop and retain motivation in staff and teams in organisations. Moreover, an appropriate reward and recognition system will have a positive correlation with behaviours of employees towards consistency in the success of Lean Six Sigma.

8

LEAN SIX SIGMA SUSTAINABILITY

8.1 INTRODUCTION

In most organisations, Lean Six Sigma (LSS) implementation kick-starts with a lot of fanfare. After two to three cycles of Lean Six Sigma projects, the program will usually start losing its momentum. Sustaining improvements for a longer duration is a common challenge in many organisations today. There are several reasons why sustaining LSS projects improvements becomes challenging. If the focus is on short-term quick wins through the execution of projects, then Lean Six Sigma programs cannot be sustained. Organisations need to think about embedding the principles of Lean Six Sigma into its DNA for sustainability, and Lean Six Sigma should be used as a catalyst to change the attitudes and behaviours of the workforce. This chapter discusses these critical sustainability challenges and a few strategies that will help managers overcome them towards sustaining Lean Six Sigma in organisations. Failing to sustain Lean Six Sigma may not only affect the returns on investments that go into developing the program but also make staff to lose interest in continuous improvement. When sustained over longer durations of time, Lean Six Sigma offers several benefits that include employee learning and satisfaction, customer satisfaction and loyalty, a culture of continuous improvement in the workplace and most importantly a competitive edge for the company. Hence, sustaining Lean Six Sigma is highly important and should be part of the leadership agenda.

8.2 TEN CRITICAL CHALLENGES IN SUSTAINING LSS IMPLEMENTATIONS

Although Lean Six Sigma has been widely accepted and applied in both manufacturing and services, there is a dearth of research on sustaining its implementations. If a management program like Lean Six Sigma is not sustained over a period of time, it may lead to incorrect conclusions by management leading to undermining its effectiveness. Hence it is important to examine the challenges in sustaining Lean Six Sigma implementations. The top ten critical challenges in sustaining LSS implementation in organisations are presented next.

1. First, it is essential to understand the nature of the sector in which Lean Six Sigma is applied. Many practitioners often employ similar strategies to deploy Lean Six Sigma with little or no importance to the sectoral context of its application. For example, Lean Six Sigma implementation in services has been significantly different from that of manufacturing due to inherent and distinct characteristics of the service industry. More precisely speaking, even within services a contextual distinction exists – pure services vs product-based services. Failure to realise the contextual differences that are unique to every sector leads to challenges in sustaining Lean Six Sigma journeys in firms.

2. In our experience, we have come across several practitioners who miss to see Lean Six Sigma from a systems perspective. When a Lean Six Sigma project is viewed narrowly its focus tends to fall on a metric improvement. Though focus on a chosen project metric is important, it is equally important to see the big picture of the overall system. At times, narrow focus on a metric could negatively influence another metric within the same process. For example, within the focus of improving accuracy, a Lean Six Sigma project cannot compromise on responsiveness of a process. Unlike project managers, business leaders do not really see individual Lean Six Sigma projects, but rather they see how the overall system and associated metrics

are performing together. When business leaders perceive Lean Six Sigma to be narrowly focussing on a metric and lose sight of the overall systemic view of the process, they may not sponsor the initiative over a long run, which leads to sustainability issues.

3. Quite often, Lean Six Sigma improves the skills, knowledge levels and abilities of the staff members during their participation in the initiative. In fact, an employee learning through problem-solving has been recognised as a positive effect of Lean Six Sigma. This learning amongst the participative staff members improves their marketability in the talent markets. Several practitioner-based surveys are a testimonial to claim that Lean Six Sigma certified staff earn more salaries than others. Hence, retaining these Lean Six Sigma trained staff members becomes challenging. Every time a firm loses its Lean Six Sigma trained staff to its competitors or other market players, the knowledge (tacit knowledge) gets diffused. This hinders the rate of maturity of Lean Six Sigma leading to issues in its sustainability.

4. While referring to Lean, Womack and Jones (2005) cautioned that if 'Lean is seen as a means of quickly cutting costs to meet budget deficits, organisations fail to achieve the real benefits'. This is equally true in the case of Lean Six Sigma. Organisations that are focused on short-term successes or quick wins may not realise Lean Six Sigma is a journey and hence naturally cannot sustain the initiative over a long run.

5. Organisational leaders play a significant role in sustaining Lean Six Sigma. For example, Jack Welch was known for his Six Sigma leadership at General Electric. But the program underwent significant changes to its downfall after his exit from the company as noted by a few reports. When there is change in leadership at the top-management level, sustaining Lean Six Sigma becomes challenging.

6. Another critical challenge in sustaining Lean Six Sigma is not aligning the continuous improvement projects with the strategic objectives of the firm. When the Lean Six Sigma strategy is

not strongly linked to organisational strategy, a few projects may show results due to mere chance. But, over a long run the Lean Six Sigma program may undergo a natural death due to lack of direction.

7. It is a well-known fact that top management's commitment is a critical success factor of Lean Six Sigma. It is not only a factor for success in implementation but also an essential ingredient for sustainability of the initiative. We have observed a few organisations where top-management personnel show a lot of interest and commitment at the initial few years of the Lean Six Sigma program, but the interest slowly fades away over a period of time, and this becomes a challenge. Management's role of providing uncompromising support needs to be consistently demonstrated for identifying, prioritising and overseeing projects.

8. Another big challenge in sustaining Lean Six Sigma is the lack of understanding its true purpose and position in relation to other technologies. When a new technology comes to the market, a few organisational leaders incorrectly assume that the new technology could replace Lean Six Sigma. The true purpose of Lean Six Sigma is to create a culture of continuous improvement and hence it is a strategic resource. Any new technology can only supplement or complement this culture but certainly cannot replace or compete with Lean Six Sigma. For example, Lean Six Sigma boosts up Industry 4.0–based technologies like Robotics Process Automations and Machine Learning. It is meaningless to automate a process that has waste and variation, and hence Lean Six Sigma should be seen as an enabler for engaging new technologies. If this philosophical essence of Lean Six Sigma is not understood correctly by organisational leaders, it leads to challenges in its sustainability.

9. It is quite natural for organisations to judge themselves as experts or market leaders in Lean Six Sigma when they achieve a certain level of maturity on continuous improvement. However, in a few cases, this thinking leads to the 'have-done-enough' attitude. In our experience of interacting with several

Master Black Belts representing a few organisations that followed Lean Sigma for several years, We found that after a few years of deployment, they start feeling that they have done enough of Lean Six Sigma and it's an old wine. This thinking in management could lead to challenges in its sustainability. A continuous improvement journey can never reach a tipping point of saturation, as the 'sky is the limit for improvement', and that is what the word 'continuous' means. It is essential for management to look at revising the Lean Six Sigma objectives periodically to keep them more challenging for an interesting journey of continuous improvement.

10. While the deployment-level challenges are critical, sustaining the gains after implementing the LSS improvements at the project level are equally important. This is where ownership becomes an essential factor for sustainability. Generally, after completing a project, the project manager (Black Belts) will be allocated to a new LSS project and hence, they do not focus any more on the completed projects. Though LSS encourages the 'Control' phase in its road map to sustain results, lack of ownership makes it unsuccessful many times. In such a scenario, the process tends to revert to its old habits leading to challenges in sustaining the benefits of Lean Six Sigma. Hence, ownership is important to sustain the results reaped from successful projects.

8.3 A FEW STRATEGIES TO OVERCOME THE CHALLENGES OF LSS SUSTAINABILITY

We present a few strategies that organisations should adopt to sustain Lean Six Sigma programs. These strategies should enable managers to overcome the previously discussed challenges in isolation or in combination. However, managers should treat these strategies as a resource, which when combined with their managerial cognition results in satisfying outcomes.

- Create a culture of consistent management commitment, leadership, accountability and participation in Lean Six Sigma programs. Leadership should realise that LSS is a 'cash cow' and as organisational leaders, they can never lose interest in LSS as it reduces costs and keeps the cash flowing. This conviction and associated behaviour have a domino effect top-down the organisational hierarchy.

- Link Lean Six Sigma to the business strategy and periodically upgrade the LSS strategy based on environmental changes and organisational maturity of LSS capability. This should involve periodic revisions in branding, involvement of the right people, executions and celebration approaches.

- Create an effective rewards and recognition program that attracts, develops and retains motivation in staff members over a period of time.

- Create a sense of urgency in purpose so that Lean Six Sigma is not an attraction factor but a hygiene factor in organisations.

- Promote total employee participation, agility and customer-centricity in Lean Six Sigma project management.

- Ensure a robust governance in project identification, prioritisation, execution and most importantly ownership of results/improvements during and post completion of the Lean Six Sigma projects.

- Invest in creating an attractive and appropriate organisational infrastructure for Lean Six Sigma. This should include training, project management, communications, market research, ideation platforms, etc.

- Ensure knowledge management of Lean Six Sigma projects is in place. Promote knowledge sharing, internalisation, externalisation and socialisation of knowledge amongst staff members. The Lean Six Sigma knowledge that emerges from the staff members' participation and experience (tacit knowledge) should be documented as much as possible (explicit knowledge).

- Organisations generally focus on sustaining the gains after implementing the LSS improvements. This is 'backward thinking'. To be effective, one should begin to focus on sustaining the improvement gains in the course of its implementation itself – otherwise, improvements are unlikely to last. In order to drive sustainability as an ongoing effort right from the improvement phase of the projects, management systems are to be put in place.

- Finally, 'institutionalisation' of LSS is essential for sustainability. Once the LSS program becomes part of the organisational DNA, the financial impact could be sustained leading to the pervasive LSS culture for transformation – even beyond the LSS practitioners and beyond the organisation boundaries.

8.4 CONCLUSIONS

An LSS program that is not sustained is considered a failure. Hence LSS sustainability is not a 'good to have' component of LSS deployment, but an 'essential' component. Having said that easily, in a real-world scenario, sustaining LSS involves significant change management, and naturally involves addressing several challenges. This chapter presented the top ten frequently occurring challenges and associated strategies to overcome them. These strategies work effectively when used along with managerial cognition, due to their context-specific effectiveness. However, the challenges and strategies presented here are not comprehensive and are based on the authors' experience. This could be a potential opportunity for research to embark exploring other possible challenges and associated strategies of sustaining LSS through an empirical validation.

9

LINKING LEAN SIX SIGMA WITH INNOVATION AND ORGANISATIONAL LEARNING

9.1 INTRODUCTION

Organisations that are subjected to accelerating change put focus on their learning ability. To have organisational learning (OL), there must also be individual learning, which puts emphasis on lifelong learning. Lean Six Sigma (LSS) is an enabler of individual learning as it promotes activity-based learning though project management and structured problem-solving. A few other aspects of OL such as social aspects, cultural aspects of human action, cognitive aspects, technical aspects of the work, change aspects, etc. are also linked with the LSS deployment (Antony, Gupta, Sunder, & Gijo, 2018).

LSS integrates the human aspects (leadership, communication, empowerment, etc.) with process performance aspects (process stability, process capability, etc.). In our experience, for the sustainability of LSS, organisations need to be equally good at both human and technical components. Anand, Ward, Tatikonda, and Schilling (2009) provide empirical evidence of the dynamic capability perspective and its underlying theory of OL for continuous improvement initiatives such as Lean and Six Sigma. Dynamic capability is the firm's ability to integrate, build and reconfigure internal competencies to address rapidly changing environments (Teece, Pisano, & Shuen, 1997). In other words, it is the ability of an organisation to reallocate or reconfigure resources to adapt to change in the future. As LSS is a problem-solving methodology, one will create knowledge and gain experience in structured problem-solving and determine the root causes of a problem with an unknown solution. As people work in teams to solve complex problems, both individuals and the team master the tools and techniques integrated in the methodology. Based on the above it can be argued that LSS enhances both individual and OL.

Another interesting topic which is under-researched is the link between LSS and innovation which includes product/process and service innovation. There are mixed views on this particular topic in the current literature. In our personal experience, we found that LSS is commonly viewed as fostering incremental innovation. LSS is not very effective for fostering radical or breakthrough innovation and in such circumstances, the authors strongly suggest that organizations invest in Design for Lean Six Sigma (DFLSS) instead of LSS. The authors will dedicate the next section on this topic and present some evidence from a recent study carried out in the UK.

9.2 LINKING LSS WITH INNOVATION

Although there are a few empirical studies available in Total Quality Management (TQM) and innovation, there are limited papers that report about the explicit relationship between LSS and innovation. Innovation can be defined as the 'introduction of new things or methods' (Random House, 1981). Innovation can be incremental/continuous, radical or disruptive. Incremental innovation is essentially an aspect of continuous improvement and this implies a series of projects that can be carried out to improve a particular process in a continuous manner. This process may include the application of basic tools and techniques and even a problem-solving methodology such as DMAIC (Define-Measure-Analyse-Improve-Control). Federal Express, when it introduced overnight mail delivery years ago, was also clearly innovative in a radical way, as no other overnight mail delivery service existed at the time, and many thought such a service would be impossible to implement (Hoerl & Gardner, 2010). Both types of innovation are required for the long-term success of any organisation. Hoerl and Gardner (2010) argued that organisations seeking long-term success will need a balanced approach to business improvement that includes methods for basic problem-solving, approaches to continuous process improvement such as LSS and also systems to identify opportunities for radical or disruptive innovation. The authors also made an interesting point that 'focusing solely in radical innovation is a recipe for financial disaster as long-term success requires a balanced approach that plays both radical innovation and continuous improvement or incremental innovation'.

The authors also have a similar view to Hoerl and Gardner (2010) that LSS is primarily a powerful methodology for improving existing processes. LSS can help organisations with incremental process innovation through problem-solving efforts; it is not designed to develop the best ideas for radical process innovation. According to Hindo (2007), LSS stifles process innovation. As LSS follows a structured and disciplined methodology using the DMAIC approach, it leads to people blindly following a rigid process. The authors would like to make a counter-argument to this point that although the methodology is standard, the use of tools and techniques in our experience are very much problem-specific. Each project is unique in its own way and therefore the application of tools from basic level to advanced level relies on the nature of the problem, the complexity around it as well as the type of industry. The DMAIC problem-solving methodology encourages creative thinking about the problem and its solution. One of the stringent assumptions of using LSS methodology is that the solution should be unknown to the person or team who tackles the problem from the outset and how someone can solve a problem without using creativity. In the Improve phase of DMAIC, the project leader encourages the team to brainstorm creative ideas which leads to potential solutions.

The following section shows empirical evidence from a study carried out to explore the relationship between LSS and innovation. The research question of interest to the study was 'Does LSS foster or hinder innovation and if it does how?' This exploratory study was conducted in 10 UK-based firms based on convenience sampling methods. The samples included manufacturing, service and professional services firms (consultancy firms). The reason for the choice of convenience sampling method was the geographical region where the research was conducted due to time and finance constraints. All the participating firms selected have been involved in LSS implementation for a minimum of three years (Antony, Setijono, & Dahlgaard, 2016).

The primary data were collected through semi-structured interviews with LSS Master Black Belts (MBBs) and Black Belts (BBs) in manufacturing, service and consultancy firms. Each participant was interviewed for an hour and the questions were related to (1) whether LSS inhibits or fosters incremental innovation and (2) the challenges faced by LSS in creating a culture of innovation. The participants of the study were reassured that their responses would be kept confidential and there were no right or wrong answers to the questions. One of the limitations of the study was that only one person from each company was involved in the research and therefore the key findings from the analysis may not be reproducible and consistent.

The majority of respondents from the companies that participated in the interview concluded that LSS does foster innovation. One of the LSS MBBs in a consulting firm indicated that LSS is adaptable for an environment where the level of innovation is high. Moreover, he also highlighted the fact that most of his clients focus on radical innovation with very little focus on incremental innovation. All interviewees agreed and recognised that LSS plays an important role in building an innovation culture. Firms with a significant service component in their offering seem to be able to foster or cultivate an Innovation culture while implementing LSS. This is because service is linked to, and dependent on, the service processes. Changes in the processes will cause changes in the delivery of service, which may appear as Innovation. Regardless of the type of firm, customers are an important driver of Innovation.

For manufacturing and hybrid companies, there are additional drivers of innovation such as technology and suppliers (Antony, Roders, et al., 2016; Antony, Setijono, et al., 2016; Antony, Vinodh, et al., 2016).

The interviewees made the following comments when they were asked about the success factors for developing a culture of innovation in companies employing LSS.

Lean Six Sigma can provide powerful tools for proper communication within the organisation and within the team, a culture of sharing and trust, open dialogue and idea sharing (LSS consultant from a consultancy firm with 9 year experience on LSS)

LSS can create a learning environment and will inculcate innovative mind in people (LSS Black Belt from a large manufacturing company with 8 year experience on LSS)

Because LSS is in place, people will improve their problem-solving skills and in the long run this will help in developing an innovative culture (Innovation manager and Black Belt from a large manufacturing company with 5 year experience on LSS)

While solving problems or finding improvement opportunities both Lean and Six Sigma methodologies openly acknowledge the importance of employee suggestions. Therefore, the existence of a proper system to gather ideas and suggestions from employees is essential for innovation. This is well aligned with the view that employee involvement is necessary in the innovation process. These results lead to the understanding that strategic LSS project selection, explorative problem-solving and employee suggestion system are perceived as having a positive influence on innovation.

In the organisations engaging with Lean Six Sigma, improvement projects are selected, executed, led and monitored by individuals in the various ranks of the 'belt' system. From the experience of a participating company (large manufacturing company) in our study, the proper institutionalisation of the 'belt' system would likely have a positive effect on innovation. To establish and institutionalise the 'belt' system, leadership, teamwork, communication and top management commitment are undeniably important (Antony, Roders, et al., 2016; Antony, Setijono, et al., 2016; Antony, Vinodh, et al., 2016).

9.3 LINKING LSS WITH ORGANISATIONAL LEARNING

In the absence of learning, companies (and individuals) simply repeat old practices. Change remains cosmetic and improvements are either fortuitous or short-lived. Business process improvement methodologies such as LSS require a commitment to learning. A learning organisation is 'an organization in which individuals and teams watch and learn, make changes, experiment, and then learn from those experiments. This should be going on every day within every team at every level' (Johnson, 1993). Based on this definition of learning organisation, LSS uses a problem-solving methodology by individuals with varied levels of expertise and they make necessary changes to the given situation so that the most effective solution can be derived. This process involves learning at individual level, team level and even at organisational level.

Several scholars view OL as a process that unfolds over time and link it with knowledge acquisition and improved performance. Many organisations have been effective at creating or acquiring new knowledge but notably less successful in applying that knowledge to their own activities (Garvin, 1993). In our experience, most organisations acquire the knowledge of LSS through good training programs but only a handful of them have a good infrastructure in place to identify LSS projects and create and share knowledge gained from both successful and unsuccessful projects. Leadership and management commitment are critical in developing the required infrastructure for problem-solving and allocating the right resources (time, people, etc.) for executing projects at both strategic and operational levels.

OL is more than individual learning and arises through individuals interacting in groups and teams of different sizes at various levels across the organisation. Learning organisations give employees the power to solve problems autonomously, as well as to benefit from the experience of their peers. They have the opportunity to share their ideas and insights without the fear of being judged, to expand their knowledge and work together to achieve common goals. The basic rationale for a learning organisation is that in situations of rapid change only those that are flexible, adaptive and productive will excel. For this to happen, it is argued, the organisation needs to 'discover how to tap employee's commitment and capacity to learn at all levels'. In the learning organisation, the ability of the organisation and its managers is not measured by what it knows (that is the product of learning), but rather by how it learns – the process of learning. Management practices encourage, recognise and reward with openness, systemic thinking, creativity and a sense of efficacy and empathy.

The following are the building blocks of a learning organisation. For more information on the detailed explanation of these building blocks, we recommend the readers to refer to the work of Garvin (1993).

- **Systematic Problem-Solving:** Problem-solving exercises should be executed based on a scientific approach rather than using gut feeling and a trial and error approach. All decision-making processes should be based on data rather than assumptions. Basic statistical tools should be used to organise data and draw inferences.

- **Experimentation:** Experiments are conducted to either explore or find something new or to test and verify an assumption. Use small well-planned experiments to produce incremental gains in knowledge.

- **Learning from past experiences:** Organisations should review both successes and failures in a systematic manner and record the key lessons learnt in a format that employees find open and accessible. Learning from failures can be quite instrumental in achieving subsequent successes, provided that organisations develop a learning mechanism from failures.

- **Learning from others:** Sometimes the most powerful insights come from looking outside one's immediate environment to gain a new perspective (Garvin, 1993). The following two methods can be extremely invaluable in our view:

    1. Other companies – Identify best-practice organisations, use site visits and interviews to study how they get work done and generate ideas for improving your own practices.

2. Your customers – Meet customers regularly to gather information about their views and opinions about the quality of service provided, understand their preferences and how well you are doing compared to your competitors.

- **Transferring Knowledge:** The way in which we transfer and receive knowledge can directly impact the company's success. One of the most simple and effective ways to transfer knowledge across any organisation is by moving the experts in their field to different departments or divisions. For instance, in the context of LSS, top talented individuals such as LSS MBBs or BBs can be transferred to various departments so that high impactful strategic projects can be executed to demonstrate the benefits of LSS in non-manufacturing areas.

The following section attempts to link LSS with OL. In the deployment of LSS, continuous improvement and learning are linked through the application of DMAIC as a problem-solving methodology. A study from Savolainen and Haikonen (2007) has shown that DMAIC is closely linked to the Deming's PDCA cycle showing a structure for dynamic continuous improvement through learning. There are two types of OL (i.e. single loop and double loop) discussed in the literature. Both types of OL are required so that the organisation and its employees will improve their understanding of the most effective way of solving problems. Single-loop learning can be described as a situation in which we observe our present situation and face problems or errors/defects. After that we adapt our own behaviour and actions to mitigate and improve the situation accordingly. In double-loop learning, we are forced to think about our actions in the framework of our operating assumptions. Double-loop learning will lead to deeper understanding of our assumptions and better decision-making in our everyday operations. In our opinion, the use of Lean thinking is single-loop learning whereas the systematic use of DMAIC for fixing problems with unknown solutions can be argued to follow double-loop learning.

The last part of this section presents empirical evidence of a study which demonstrates the relationship between LSS and OL (Sony & Naik, 2012). A survey was carried out across Indian companies representing East, West, North and South India. The questionnaire was primarily targeted at senior managers in each company and a total of 495 responses were received. The key findings of the study are as follows:

- The Six Sigma role structure is positively related to OL. This means organisations develop process improvement specialists such as LSS BBs and Green Belts through intensive training and execution of process improvement projects, which after the training will contribute to OL. The use of well-disciplined and systematic methodology along with relevant tools and techniques with the projects and working towards certain process performance goals set in the define phase also contribute to OL.

- The Six Sigma focus on role structure and metrics positively impact on the organisation innovation. Similar views were expressed by Caroline and Raghu (2009) where they stated that innovation requires the coordinated efforts of many skilled actors and this is clearly the case with the execution of LSS projects.

- The study shows no evidence of organisation type exerting a moderating effect on the impact of Lean Six Sigma on OL. Further research should be pursued exploring how different types of organisations (i.e. both size and nature) implementing LSS have an impact on OL.

9.4 SUMMARY

This chapter explores the relationship between LSS, innovation and OL. Lean Six Sigma role structure, Lean Six Sigma structured improvement methodology and focus on Lean Six Sigma metrics enhance commitment to learning, shared vision and open-mindedness, thereby promoting OL. Leaders in organisations play an important role in linking LSS with innovation and OL. Good leaders will create a context whereby culture nurtures the development of both innovation and learning capabilities. The essence of exceptional organisations implementing LSS is about their ability to sustain competitiveness through the continuous pursuit of innovation and learning.

10

LINKING LEAN SIX SIGMA WITH GREEN AND ENVIRONMENTAL SUSTAINABILITY

10.1 INTRODUCTION

Lean Six Sigma enables waste elimination and defect reduction. As manufacturing and service systems are becoming environmentally sustainable, Lean Six Sigma needs to be integrated with green technology and environmental sustainability tools to enable environmental and operational benefits. The purpose of this chapter is to provide this linking perspective of Lean Six Sigma. Understanding this perspective is important for contemporary managers. Primarily, with the changing business challenges and importance for the triple bottom line, it is important for managers to balance all three types of sustainability, namely economic, environmental and social. Thus, firms have to account for the resources they use and the resulting footprint they leave behind (owing to activities such as production, transportation, recycling and remanufacturing of current products and the design of new products). Second, companies need to operate in a sagacious and responsible manner and take care of employee health and safety, and quality of life of the external community (Gimenez, Sierra, & Rodon, 2012). Thus linking Lean Six Sigma with Green technology towards realising sustainability benefits becomes important.

10.2 GREEN LEAN SIX SIGMA AND ENVIRONMENTAL SUSTAINABILITY

Green technology is an approach that aims to eliminate/minimise wastes in a system towards minimising negative effects on the environmental. It recommends three strategies for this purpose – recycle, reuse and reduce, towards reducing negative ecological impacts and optimising resource efficiency. It contributes positively on people, planet and profitability of the industries by reducing adverse environmental affects and through optimum use of available resources. Blending this essential Green technology with Lean and Six Sigma offers novel approaches to minimise waste generation through the reduction of process variation, called Green Lean Six Sigma. The customer-centric Six Sigma approach brings in the flavour of variation reduction; the Lean approach fiercely advocates the systematic removal of non-value-added activities; and the Green approach reduces the negative environmental impact of the process and product by making it more ecofriendly. Thus, Green Lean Six Sigma is more powerful and enhances the original Green technology.

Let us understand this term 'Green Lean Six Sigma' step by step. First, Lean and Green have several things in common. For example, the seven deadly wastes of Lean have parallels in Green technology. Table 10.1 summarises these similarities. One similarity between these two approaches is the focus on optimising resource efficiency. Another similarity is their purposes through which they complement each other for synergies. While Lean may not have a direct intent to reduce environmental impact, lean thinking can potentially improve organisational productivity and environmental performance.

While they share several similarities, Lean and Green do not tackle the issue of variation in products and its associated impact on the environment. Thus, the Lean Green approach mainly encompasses practices like Green supply chain, reverse logistics, 5S, mistake proofing, Green building, that are all not capable of producing a product or service of true value even though Lean Green can produce a product that meets customer specifications. Thus, the integration of Six Sigma with Lean Green becomes essential. The principal idea behind integrating Six Sigma and Lean Green is that if

Table 10.1. Linking Lean Green – Similarity in Views.

	Type of Waste	Lean View	Green View
1	Transportation	Unnecessary movement of goods from one place to another	Leads to fossil or other forms of energy consumption
2	Inventory	Hides process-related problems and obstructs communication between people	Inventory demands storage and security, which consume energy
3	Motion	Unnecessary movement of people or information	Opportunity for different forms of pollution, an associated consequence on environment
4	Waiting Time	Leads to underutilisation of full capacity	Wasted energy in various forms (through associated infrastructure) during the wait time
5	Over Processing	Efforts wasted in refining more than required	Consumption of energy resources in the production of extra material that increase environmental effects
6	Over Production	Efforts wasted in refining more than required leading to inventory	Leads to unhealthy ambience within the work place
7	Defects	That which does not meet the customer expectations	Rework associated to correct defects, consuming extra energy

the imperfections in a process can be measured, then the solution can be planned to eliminate them. While the Six Sigma methodology reduces process inconsistencies, it will not be able to reduce the wastes causing environmental damage via the associated process (Garza-Reyes, 2015). Thus, Green, Lean and Six Sigma together become powerful as each of them compensates for each other's limitations towards creating a synergetic approach. Lean, Green and Six Sigma have a positive effect on environmental performance in terms of waste reduction, and the resulting reduced process variation leads to consumption of lesser raw material, energy, rework and scrap which in turns reduces the impact on the environment (Ruben, Vinodh, & Asokan, 2017). Hence Green Lean Six Sigma has great potential to become part of leadership agenda in organisations.

10.3 CHALLENGES AND THE EMERGING TREND OF INTEGRATION OF GREEN LEAN SIX SIGMA

While the construct Green Lean Six Sigma is both essential and has potential benefits for organisations, its implementation constitutes several challenges. First, not all organisations care about the environment. Though the regulatory and government-imposed rules govern or direct organisations to focus on environmentally friendly processes, products and services, most of the environmental improvement projects fall by the wayside because by themselves they are not viewed as significant enough to capture management's attention and gain a share of the organisation's limited capital and resources. Second, environment management systems are generally kept as a stand-alone system outside the LSS agenda. In other words, these two initiatives are managed independently by management and thus there is little or no opportunity for practical integration naturally. Further, even the most reputed certification systems like the International Organization for Standardization (ISO) recommends two different certification standards – ISO 9001 for Quality Management Systems and ISO 14001 for Environment Management Systems. While there is much overlap with many similar or identical requirements between these standards, they still remain to be two different certifications.

There are different ways organisations could get them on the same platform for both economic and environmental benefits. The benefits of creating projects that are both environmentally focused and LSS compliant are not just theory. While a few organisations focus on these challenges, several other organisations started combining projects as they are more appealing because they can claim to pay both environmental and quality improvement dividends. In LSS projects, efforts are taken to minimise the negative impacts on air quality, water quality and ecosystem in addition to the activities that provide process improvements. This would enable firms to reduce its basic resource consumption and thus enable reduction of its operational costs. In our experience, We have come across corporations with a commitment to environmental preservation along with a focus on the bottom line. A few examples:

- A global development bank realised 150 million USD saved by reducing food wastage in their corporate dining areas by deploying a Lean Six Sigma program. The project scope included 175 countries, among which more than 40% of the countries had a significant food wastage problem. The project involved data collection of solid and liquid food separately, analysing the root causes and ideating for novel solutions. Variety, quality and quantity were the primary causes found during the project which were varying across different days of the week. The LSS project team used visual management boards, employee self-selection of food menu options, etc. as solutions to solve the issue.

- An American multinational conglomerate conducted over 200 energy audits to identify waste in its worldwide facilities, resulting in several LSS projects. This effort reduced greenhouse gas emissions by 250,000 metric tons and saved $70 million in energy costs.

- A healthcare facility analysed its water use and developed an action plan to save 170,000 gallons of water per day and 17,000 USD within three months. This project required value stream mapping and Kaizen events and eliminated the need to expand its wastewater treatment plant.

10.4 CONCLUSIONS

With the increasing attention towards sustainable operations and sustainable development, organisations should realise the importance of the environment. Balancing economic growth with a sense of responsibility towards the environment is thus needed. Thinking beyond regulatory and government-imposed norms for the environment should be self-motivated organisational initiatives. With the 2010 publication of an international standard on social responsibility (ISO 26000), and increased attention to sustainability and sustainability reporting, many organisations today are following this call. In this chapter, we have introduced this perspective to think on LSS projects and associate deployments beyond operational benefits. We hope our conceptualisation helps managers balance both economic and environmental sustainability. Future research should focus on developing new models, frameworks and implications towards this thinking.

11

BEYOND LSS: EMERGING THEMES OF LEAN SIX SIGMA

11.1 INTRODUCTION

Much has changed and much has been accomplished in the world since Six Sigma was introduced by Motorola in the mid-1980s. Many organisations around the globe, large and small, have used first Six Sigma and now Lean Six Sigma (LSS) to become more successful: quality has been improved, delivery times have been reduced, waste has been decreased and customer satisfaction has been enhanced (Antony, Snee, & Hoerl, 2017). An important by-product of this work has been saving billions of dollars around the world. LSS has benefitted organisations of all types including manufacturing, service, healthcare, government, non-profits and education (McKeon et al., 2010). The expansion of the LSS methodology and application of the approach to improvement will continue as new needs and opportunities are encountered.

The future of LSS depends on the improvement needs of the organisations involved. The continuing and emerging trends creating these needs and opportunities include:

- Integration of LSS with Robotic Process Automation
- Integration of LSS with Big Data
- LSS within a holistic improvement strategy and methodology

- Integration of LSS with Statistical Engineering
- Lean Six Sigma in Public Sector organisations
- Integration of LSS into higher educational systems

These trends create the need for better strategies to target improvement opportunities. The LSS methodology will also have to be improved to successfully deal with these opportunities. The authors will provide a detailed explanation of each theme outlined above, and we anticipate these themes will continually progress over the years to come.

11.2 INTEGRATION OF LSS WITH ROBOTIC PROCESS AUTOMATION

Robotic Process Automation or RPA is one of the most recent automation technologies to emerge and uses software robots to mimic the actions a human user would perform on a computer application in order to automate business processes that are highly repetitive and rule-based (primarily back office tasks such as sending invoices). RPA is very useful for automating existing processes in organisations especially when they are operated by a number of staff members. However, individuals should be cautious prior to making massive investments on this technology. The authors strongly recommend utilising 'Lean Thinking' in existing processes so that waste and cycle times can be reduced prior to investing on RPA. In many cases, the existing business processes are overly complex with non-valued steps that could be eliminated before RPA is implemented.

An excellent example on the integration of LSS and RPA was illustrated in the work of Davenport and Brain (2018). The example was taken from a multinational company known as the world's largest payroll and HR services provider. In order to improve the efficiency of processes across the business, it has adopted LSS. Combining the capabilities of RPA with the LSS way of working was a natural fit. It enables standardised waste-free automated processes, delivered at a speed and cost point, which is much more advantageous than other automation technologies, thereby extending improvements. According to the VP of business process improvement (BPI) at the company under discussion *'the majority of BPI projects in the future will involve RPA, the focus is on the process optimisation first to make sure that we identify the areas for improvement within a process, analyse the process and improve it using the tools and techniques of LSS and finally automate it'*.

It is important to note that automation won't save a badly designed process. Therefore, it is crucial that your RPA journey starts with some process modelling efforts. The best way to do that is by applying the basic tools of Lean including value stream mapping, waste analysis, standard operating procedures, etc. There are numerous benefits one can gain from the integration of LSS with RPA. Some of the typical benefits from the integrated approach include:

- **Freeing up staff for high value tasks:** For example, when assessing an insurance claim, more time can be spent in the assessment as opposed to populating the same data into five various systems. However, the focus of Lean Six Sigma is to streamline the assessment process in the eyes of customers and reduce defects in the assessment process prior to applying RPA.

- **Reduced operational risk:** RPA reduces the rate of errors because robots make less mistakes. Avoiding or minimising human errors from tiresome due to repetitive tasks means a lower level of operational risk.

- **Reduced variability in output performance:** As similar tasks are carried out in a consistent manner with the use of RPA, a superior consistency in process outputs can be achieved. However, the LSS methodology (DMAIC) could be utilised initially to reduce process variability prior to investing RPA.

- **Improved customer experience:** One of the greatest benefits of employing RPA is to free up some of the skilled employees (who have been constantly dealing with repetitive tasks) and put them back on the front line dealing with customer problems and provide customers an improved experience.

- **Increased output:** Customers of today want to interact with service providers 24/7, and RPA allows organisations to deliver high-quality service with great consistency.

11.3 INTEGRATION OF LSS WITH BIG DATA

Big Data refers to complex and large data sets that have to be processed and analysed to uncover valuable information that can benefit businesses and organisations. Big Data has one or more of the following characteristics: high volume (here, volume is the amount of data generated that must be understood to make data-based decisions), high velocity (here, velocity is how fast data are produced and modified at the speed with which they need to be processed) or high variety (here, variety defines data coming from new sources – both inside and outside of an organisation). Big Data may come from sensors, devices, video/audio, networks, log files, transactional applications, web and social media — much of it generated in real time and at a very large scale.

Big Data Analytics (BDA) examines large amounts of data to uncover hidden patterns, market trends, customer preferences, unknown casualty and correlations and other insights. With today's technology, it's possible to analyse your data and get answers from them almost immediately – an effort that's slower and less efficient with more traditional business intelligence solutions. Today, organisations have a number of distributed data sources from their suppliers to the customers, and these data can be divided into different forms ranging from text, numeric, web logs, videos, tweets, etc. and become difficult to interpret and make an informed decision for many businesses. Some of the benefits from the use of BDA include:

- Better decision-making
- Improved productivity
- Reduced costs
- Improved customer service
- Greater innovation with new products and services in the market
- Faster time to market

The Big Data revolution is breathing new life into Lean and Six Sigma methodologies. In effect, it provides opportunities into a data-rich realm of reasoning that can unlock infinite efficiencies and savings when approached in the right way. Big Data offers prospects for CI professionals to solve problems previously thought to be unsolvable. While much progress has been made in medical research and Internet marketing, one area overlooked to date is the use of Big Data in the design and improvement of products, services and process quality. Customer surveys (i.e. capturing the voice of the customer) can help us better understand customer needs and experiences. The collection of manufacturing data and integrating it with customer data can help improve products and processes.

We will now provide a simple example where LSS and Big Data can work together. In a hospital setting, Big Data can include digital patient records that store a vast amount of information regarding number of visits made to the doctor, medications taken, the change of medication doses and different types of procedures undergone over a period of time. Healthcare data also include information on wait time for patients, machine idle times (CT scan, X-ray, etc.), time spent by medical staff on procedures which can be done by administrative staff, medical staff looking for charts or information of patients, time spent by doctors and consultants on unnecessary paperwork, etc. Lean Six Sigma tools can help tackle many of the above problems and provides a systematic method for developing practical solutions. The LSS methodology helps people in organisations to understand the process better and assist project leaders and teams in problem-solving scenarios to understand and verify the root causes of a problem. The integration of BDA with LSS in these situations can help LSS professionals solve problems faster. In addition to that, one can search for trends in the data and explore further analysis of data for hidden problems at no additional cost.

In a typical problem-solving scenario using the LSS methodology, we use small sample sizes to unlock the knowledge. Big Data can play a vital role here as we can use relatively huge data and look for trends, patterns or any relationship between the key process variables to unlock the knowledge. The use of data analytics methods at every stage of the DMAIC methodology, especially in the measure and analyse stages, has critical importance to make powerful decisions. In other words, the integration of LSS with Big Data can result in faster, reliable, effective and meaningful decisions. In our experience, Lean Six Sigma and Big Data can complement each other well when used properly. Big Data is not as effective without Lean Six Sigma and Lean Six Sigma is sub-optimised without Big Data.

11.4 LSS WITHIN A HOLISTIC IMPROVEMENT STRATEGY AND METHODOLOGY

It is quite evident that LSS is no longer adequate for the improvements that organisations need to survive and, better yet, prosper. All problems in businesses cannot be tackled using Lean and Six Sigma approaches to process improvement. This implies we need to select the right methodology for a specific project, rather than relying on one methodology for all problems. This justifies the need for the development of a holistic approach to process improvement in problem-solving scenarios. A holistic improvement is defined as 'an improvement system that can successfully create and sustain significant improvements of any type, in any culture, for any business' (Snee, 2009). Here 'create and sustain' refer to infrastructure – management systems and resources, CI culture, leadership development and related issues. 'Significant improvements' refer to improving performance as measured quality, cost, delivery and customer satisfaction in a way that improves the bottom line. 'Any type of improvement' refers to improving any measure of performance including flow, variation, optimisation, design, improvement and control. 'Any culture' refers to any country around the globe and any function within an organisation. 'Any organisation' refers to manufacturing, service, public sector, third sector, etc. (Antony, Rodgers, et al., 2017; Antony, Snee, et al., 2017).

The following are characteristics of holistic improvement (Snee & Hoerl, 2018):

- Works in all areas of business – all functions, all processes
- Works in all cultures
- Can address all measures of performance (cost, quality, delivery and customer satisfaction)

- Can address all types of process problems using various types of methodologies or application of just tools/techniques (e.g. some problems can be tackled using simple common sense and you do not need Lean or Six Sigma methodology, some problems can be fixed using a basic Kaizen approach with relevant people on board, etc.)
- Can address all types of improvements (cycle time reduction, waste reduction, throughput yield improvement, process capability improvement, process stability issues, setup time reduction, duplication of efforts in administration, excessive and non-productive meetings, etc.)

Sometimes a larger complex problem needs to be broken down into a number of projects, instead of tackling the whole problem using one methodology and partially solving the problem. In such cases, the authors recommend a holistic approach and use a different set of methodologies and set of tools and techniques after the problem is broken down into sub-problems.

11.5 INTEGRATION OF LSS WITH STATISTICAL ENGINEERING

Statistical Engineering (SE) includes components of strategic statistical thinking (to identify the opportunities within an organisation), tactical integration and adaptation of methods to the specific problem, and operational implementation of the specific tools and methodologies to create the required solution (Anderson-Cook & Lu, 2012). The focus of SE is on solving large unstructured high-impact problems by integrating multiple tools. These high-impact problems would be helpful to elevate influence and create more exposure of SE, which can be beneficial for SE development and securing leadership support. LSS is not suited for tackling complex and unstructured problems. The tools and concepts of SE along with Information Technology (IT) as a discipline can be integrated into the LSS methodology to achieve enhanced results. Apart from IT, other disciplines such as operations research (OR), engineering, economics, etc. might also be key, depending on the nature of the problem to be tackled. All problems require some degree of knowledge of root causes and context before tackling them. However, for complex and unstructured problems, the roots are deeper and more intricate. No textbook solution works for scenarios like above and one may need to use creative thinking to help identify the best approach (Snee & Hoerl, 2018).

The following section briefly presents an example of the use of SE combined with the LSS methodology. A large US printing company faced productivity improvement challenges and used an integrated approach of SE with LSS as a solution for tackling the challenge (Schall, 2012). The methodology engaged operations teams to establish a standard process, identify and eliminate sources of variability within their control (stabilise the process), establish the daily disciplines necessary to sustain the improvements over time and create an environment to facilitate step-change productivity improvement through Lean Six Sigma projects. The statistical and non-statistical tools of variability reduction were sequenced to enable operations teams to learn the tools and methods and to quickly attack sources of variation within their daily control. Over the course of four years, the company witnessed a 4–10% increase in sustained throughput of its manufacturing assets and evidence of improvement in their Six Sigma deployment.

11.6 LSS IN PUBLIC SECTOR ORGANISATIONS

The public sector is a significant part of the economy of any country in the world and, regardless of specific function or service or country of operation, has many challenges and operating restrictions in common. Public sector services are informed and directed by political policies and priorities which can be changeable. They compete for a share of an overall budget and must deliver their services within the affordability of budget, and this is a key consideration in the strategic management of public sector services (Rodgers & Antony, 2019).

In order to give a context to the size of the public sector, 17% of all employed individuals in the UK work in the public sector (Antony, Rodgers, et al., 2017). The Organisation for Economic Co-operation and Development (2015) shows that public sector employment ranges from up to 30% in some Scandinavian countries to as low as 8% in Japan. When considering the financial cost of the public sector, the UK Central Government received £53.6 billion in income in February 2016 (Office of National Statistics, 2016a, 2016b) and spent £57.1 billion. Approximately two-thirds of this income were through central government departments such as health, education and defence.

Recent research on LSS in Public Sector organisations has shown that there is clearly an increase in the number of publications recently and an apparent increase in the interest of the use of Lean Six Sigma in the public sector in the last few years (Rodgers & Antony, 2019). It is noted, however, that the increase appears to be Continuous Improvement (CI) practitioners and academics developing an interest in the public sector rather than the public sector-focussed researchers developing an interest in CI. Lean has been a dominant topic compared to Six Sigma and LSS for many years, and most papers have been related to the healthcare sector.

We would argue that the application is more widely spread than many people realise, but there has not yet been an evidential base showing exactly how beneficial the use of Lean Six Sigma in the public service has been to date. Additionally, activity has been delivered on a piecemeal basis which can lead to a feeling that it is a management fad carried out by consultants or specialists rather than sustainable and good practice in delivering public services across the entire gamut of the sector in the UK (Antony, Roders, & Gijo, 2016). In our personal view, Lean Six Sigma is valid for the public sector as evidenced by the myriad of individual projects being undertaken across a range of sectors including healthcare, Higher Education, local councils, Police Force, etc. The key question from that is how the public sector works together in a way that maximises benefits, reduces duplication and delivers a customer-focused and integrated service. There is clear evidence of pockets of willingness and good practice, but this needs coordination and encouragement.

11.7 INTEGRATION OF LSS INTO HIGHER EDUCATIONAL SYSTEMS

Our research over the years have shown that only a handful number of universities are engaged in Operational Excellence research topics, in particular, Six Sigma and LSS. Many universities do not offer Lean and Six Sigma courses in the curriculum of engineering and business schools, and these are the most widely accepted and adopted methodologies for achieving operational and service excellence in many organisations today. Some universities offer Lean and Six Sigma courses to industry which results in Six Sigma Green Belt and Black Belt certifications. A handful number of universities offer MSc in Operations Excellence (Cranfield), MSc in LSS for Operational Excellence (Heriot-Watt University), MSc in Lean Operations (Cardiff) and MSc in Lean Enterprise (University of Buckingham) (Sunder, 2016). In order to create Operational Excellence leaders of tomorrow, more universities should offer undergraduate and postgraduate courses in Operational and Service Excellence topics. The authors also like to suggest universities offer a compulsory course on Operational and Service Excellence to all undergraduate and postgraduate students irrespective of their discipline. This could lead to the execution of group projects that are carried out by students and improve business processes in their respective faculties (Sunder & Antony, 2018). This could lead to LSS Yellow Belt or Green Belt for students depending upon the scope of the project, nature of the problem, utilisation of tools in the problem-solving methodology and financial savings generated from the project. Three of the co-authors in the book have been heavily involved in the promotion of LSS in Higher Education sector through an International Conference over the past five years. The primary objective of the conference is to transform Higher Education Institutions (HEIs) from separate reactive operations, which are generally functionally oriented, into cross-functional process-focused organisations to meet the demands of twenty-first-century education. The conference also aims to highlight that both Lean and Six Sigma have an immense and critical role to play in creating a customer-centric approach for higher education through LSS business process improvement strategy to better fulfil the educational mission.

REFERENCES

Akao, Y. (1991). *Hoshin Kanri: Policy deployment for successful TQM*. Barrington, MA: Steiner Books.

Albliwi, S., Antony, J., Halim Lim, S. A., & van der Wiele, T. (2014). Critical failure factors of Lean Six Sigma: A systematic literature review. *International Journal of Quality & Reliability Management*, 31(9), 1012–1030.

Alefari, M., Salonitis, K., & Xu, Y. (2017). The role of leadership in implementing lean manufacturing. *Procedia CIRP*, 63, 756–761.

American Society for Quality. (2019). Six Sigma Master Black Belt certification. ASQ. Retrieved from https://asq.org/cert/master-black-belt. Accessed on May 18, 2019.

Anand, G., Ward, P. T., Tatikonda, M. V., & Schilling, D. A. (2009). Dynamic capabilities through continuous improvement infrastructure. *Journal of Operations Management*, 27(6), 444–461.

Anderson-Cook, C. M., & Lu, L. (Eds.), Panellists: Clark, G., DeHart, S. P., Hoerl, R., Jones, B., MacKay, J., Montgomery, D., … Wilson, A. G. (2012). Statistical engineering—Roles for statisticians and the path forward. *Quality Engineering*, 24(2), 133–152.

Angelis, J., Conti, R., Cooper, C., & Gill, C. (2011). Building high-commitment lean culture. *Journal of Manufacturing Technology Management*, 22(5), 569–586.

Antony, J. (2015). The ten commandments of quality: A performance perspective. *International Journal of Productivity and Performance Management*, 64(5), 723–735.

Antony, J., & Gupta, S. (2019). Top ten reasons for process improvement project failures. *International Journal of Lean Six Sigma*, 10(1), 367–374.

Antony, J., Gupta, S., Sunder, V. M., & Gijo, E. V. (2018). Ten commandments of Lean Six Sigma: A practitioners' perspective. *International Journal of Productivity and Performance Management*, 67(6), 1033–1044.

Antony, J., Roders, B., & Gijo, E. V. (2016). Can LSS make UK public sector organisations more efficient and effective? *International Journal of Prodctivity and Performance Management*, 65(7), 995–1002.

Antony, J., Setijono, D., & Dahlgaard, J. J. (2016). Lean Six Sigma and innovation – An exploratory study among UK organisations. *Total Quality Management & Business Excellence*, 27(1–2), 124–140.

Antony, J., & Snee, R. D. (2010). Leading role. *Quality Progress*, May, pp. 6–12.

Antony, J., Snee, R. D., & Hoerl, R. W. (2017). Lean Six Sigma: Yesterday, today and tomorrow. *International Journal of Quality & Reliability Management*, 34(7), 1073–1093.

Antony, J., Vinodh, S., & Gijo, E. V. (2016). *Lean Six Sigma for small and medium sized enterprises: A practical guide*. Boca Raton, FL: CRC Press.

Argyris, C. (1999). *On organizational learning*. Cambridge: Blackwell Publishers.

Arthur, W., Bennett, W., Edens, P. S., & Bell, S. T. (2003). Effectiveness of training in organizations: A meta-analysis of design and evaluation features. *Journal of Applied Psychology*, 88(2), 234–245.

Baedecke Yllner, E., & Brunila, A. (2013). *Talent management: Retaining and managing technical specialists in a technical career*. Master thesis, KTH Royal Institute of Technology, Stockholm. Retrieved from https://docplayer.net/742834-Talent-management-retaining-and-managing-technical-specialists-in-a-technical-career-emelie-baedecke-yllner-alexandra-brunila.html. Accessed on April 17, 2019.

Bass, B. (1990). From transactional to transformational leadership: Learning to share the vision. *Organizational Dynamics*, 18(3), 19–31.

Becker, B. A., Huselid, M. A., & Beatty, R. W. (2009). *The differentiated workforce: Transforming talent into strategic impact*. Boston, MA: Harvard Business Press.

Bertel, T. (2003). Integrating lean and Six Sigma – the power of an integrated roadmap. Retrieved from www.isixsigma.com. Accessed on June 20, 2019.

Bertels, T. (2003). *Rath and Strong's Six Sigma leadership handbook* (edited). Hoboken, NJ: John Wiley & Sons.

Bhuiyan, N., Baghel, A., & Wilson, J. (2006). A sustainable continuous improvement methodology at an aerospace company. *International Journal of Productivity and Performance Management*, 55(8), 671–687.

Brice, Z. (2002). *The importance of project selection: Why Six Sigma project falters, how to assure success and sustainability*. White Paper. Six Sigma Qualtec, Princeton, NJ. Retrieved from www.ssqi.com/breakthroughs/whitepaper-pdfs/Project_selection_WP.pdf. Accessed on May 2019.

Brotherton, R., & Leslie, D. (1991). Critical information needs for achieving strategic goals. In R. Teare & A. Boer (Eds.), *Strategic hospitality management: Theory and practice for the 1990's* (pp. 33–44). London: Cassell.

Brown, J. (2015). Top 5 skills of a Six Sigma practitioner. GreyCampus. Retrieved from https://www.greycampus.com/blog/quality-management/top-five-skills-of-a-six-sigma-practitioner. Accessed on May 31, 2019.

Bugay, F. (2016). Boost your company's performance with Hoshin Kanri method. Retrieved from https://www.linkedin.com/pulse/boost-your-companys-performance-hoshin-kanri-method-ferhan-bugay/

Bullen, C. V., Rockart, J. F., & No, S. W. (1981). II. Definitions and concepts III. Interview procedure and data analysis technique. In *A primer on critical success factors*.

Burns, J. M. (1978). *Leadership*. New York, NY: Harper & Row.

Caroline, A. B., & Raghu, G. (2009). The role of narratives in sustaining organizational innovation. *Organization Science*, 20(1), 107–117.

CEB. (2014). The HR guide to identifying high-potentials. CEB SHL Talent Measurement. Retrieved from http://www.ucop.edu/human-resources/management-development-program/2014/Donna%20Handout.pdf

Chambers, E. G., Foulon, M., Handfield-Jones, H., Hankin, S. M., & Michaels, E. G. (1998). The war for talent. *McKinsey Quarterly, 3,* 44–57.

Cherrafi, A., Elfezazi, S., Govindan, K., Garza-Reyes, J. A., Benhida, K., & Mokhlis, A. (2017). A framework for the integration of Green and Lean Six Sigma for superior sustainability performance. *International Journal of Production Research, 55*(15), 4481–4515.

Collins, J. (2001). *Good to great.* New York, NY: HarperCollins.

Corbett, L. M. (2011). Lean Six Sigma: The contribution to business excellence. *International Journal of Lean Six Sigma, 2*(2), 118–131.

Covey, S. R., Merrill, A. R., & Merrill, R. R. (1997). *First things first every day: Daily reflections-because where you're headed is more important than how fast you get there.* New York, NY: Simon & Schuster.

Cudney, E., & Keim, E. (2017). The changing role of quality in the future: Required competencies for quality professionals to succeed. *Journal for Quality and Participation, 39*(4), 4–11.

Cudney, E., Sandilya, S., Materla, T., & Antony, J. (2019). Systematic review of lean six sigma approaches in higher education. *Total Quality Management & Business Excellence,* 1–14. doi:10.1080/14783363.2017.1422977

Daniel, D. R. (1961). Management information crisis. *Harvard Business Review,* September/October, pp. 111–120.

Davenport, T. H., & Brain, D. (2018). Before automating your company's processes, find ways to improve them. *Harvard Business Review,* June. Retrieved from https://hbr.org/2018/06/before-automating-your-companys-processes-find-ways-to-improve-them. Accessed on July 19, 2019.

Devlin, G. (1989). How to implement a winning strategy. *European Management Journal, 7*(3), 377–383.

Eckes, G. (2003). *Six Sigma for everyone.* New York, NY: John Wiley & Sons.

Finch, C. R., & Crunkilton, J. R. (1999). *Curriculum development in vocational and technical education: Planning, content, and implementation.* Needham, MA: Allyn & Bacon.

Gagné, M., & Deci, E. L. (2005). Self-determination theory and work motivation. *Journal of Organizational Behavior*, 26(4), 331–362.

Gardiner, J. J. (2006). Transactional, transformational, and transcendent leadership: Metaphors mapping the evolution of the theory and practice of governance. *Leadership Review*, 6, 62–76.

Garvin, D. (1993). Building a learning organisation. *Harvard Business Review*, 71(4 (July–August)), 78–91.

Garza-Reyes, J. A. (2015). Green lean and the need for Six Sigma. *International Journal of Lean Six Sigma*, 6(3), 226–248.

George, M. L. (2002). *Lean Six Sigma: Combining Six Sigma quality with lean production speed*. New York, NY: McGraw-Hill.

George, M. L. (2003). *Lean Six Sigma for service* (p. 273). New York, NY: McGraw-Hill.

Gijo, E. V., & Rao, T. S. (2005). Six Sigma implementation – Hurdles and more hurdles. *Total Quality Management*, 16(6), 721–725.

Gimenez, C., Sierra, V., & Rodon, J. (2012). Sustainable operations: Their impact on the triple bottom line. *International Journal of Production Economics*, 140(1), 149–159.

Goleman, D., Boyatzis, R., & McKee, A. (2002). *The new leaders: Transforming the art of leadership*. London: Little Brown and Company.

Greenleaf, R. (1977). *Servant leadership – A journey into the nature of legitimate power and greatness*. New York, NY: Paulist Press.

Harlen, W., & James, M. (1997). Assessment and learning: Differences and relationships between formative and summative assessment. *Assessment in Education: Principles, Policy & Practice*, 4(3), 365–379.

Hindo, B. (2007). 3M's innovation crisis: How Six Sigma almost smothered its idea culture. *Business Week*, June 11.

Ho, Y. C., Chang, O. C., & Wang, W. B. (2008). An empirical study of key success factors for Six Sigma Green Belt projects at an Asian MRO company. *Journal of Air Transport Management*, 14(5), 263–269.

Hoerl, R. W. (2001). Six Sigma Black Belts: What do they need to know? *Journal of Quality Technology, 33*(4), 391–406. doi:10.1080/ 00224065.2001.11980094

Hoerl, R. W., & Gardner, M. M. (2010). Lean Six Sigma, creativity and innovation. *International Journal of Lean Six Sigma, 1*(1), 30–38.

Ingle, S., & Roe, W. (2001). Six sigma black belt implementation. *The TQM Magazine, 13*(4), 273–280.

Johnson, K. W. (1993). The learning organization: What is it? Why become one? Navran Associates' Newsletter.

Juran, J. M., Bigliazzi, M., Mirandola, R., Spaans, C., & Dunuad, M. (1995). "A history of managing for quality". *Quality Progress, 28*(8), 125–129.

Juran, J. M. (Ed.). (1995). *A history of managing for quality: The evolution, trends, and future directions of managing for quality*. Milwaukee, WI: ASQC Quality Press.

Ketelhohn, W. (1998). What is a key success factor? *European Management Journal, 16*(3), 335–340.

Kirkpatrick, S. A., & Locke, E. A. (1991). Leadership: Do traits matter? *The Executive, 5*(2), 48–60.

Kotter, J. P. (2008). *Force for change: How leadership differs from management*. New York, NY: Simon & Schuster.

Krafcik, J. F. (1988). Triumph of the lean production system. *Sloan Management Review, 30*(1), 41–52.

Kumar, M., Antony, J., & Cho, B. R. (2009). Project selection and its impact on the successful deployment of Six Sigma. *Business Process Management Journal, 15*(5), 669–686.

Laureani, A., & Antony, J. (2017). Leadership characteristics for Lean Six Sigma. *Total Quality Management & Business Excellence, 28*(3–4), 405–426.

Laureani, A., & Antony, J. (2018). Leadership – A critical success factor for the effective implementation of Lean Six Sigma. *Total Quality Management & Business Excellence, 29*(5–6), 502–523.

Laureani, A., & Antony, J. (2019). Leadership and Lean Six Sigma: A systematic literature review. *Total Quality Management & Business Excellence*, 30(1–2), 53–81.

Laux, C., Johnson, M., & Cada, P. (2015). Project barriers to Green Belts through critical success factors. *International Journal of Lean Six Sigma*, 6(2), 138–160.

Leidecker, J. K., & Bruno, A. V. (1984). Identifying and using critical success factors. *Long Range Planning*, 17, 23–32.

Lewin, K., Lippitt, R., & White, R. K. (1939). Patterns of aggressive behavior in experimentally created social climates. *The Journal of Social Psychology*, 10(2), 269–299.

Liker, J. K., & Convis, G. L. (2012). *The Toyota way to lean leadership: Achieving and sustaining excellence through leadership development*. New York, NY: McGraw-Hill.

Macleod, C. (2018, September 14). The true cost of hiring the wrong person. Chandler Macleod Group. Retrieved from https://www.chandlermacleod.com/blog/true-cost-hiring-wrong-person/

Mann, D. (2009). The missing link: Lean leadership. *Frontiers of Health Services Management*, 26(1), 15–26.

Mann, D. (2014). *Creating a lean culture: Tools to sustain lean conversions*. Boca Raton, FL: CRC Press.

Martin, A. (2015). Talent management: Preparing a "ready" agile workforce. *International Journal of Pediatrics and Adolescent Medicine*, 2, 112–116. Retrieved from https://www.infona.pl/resource/bwmeta1.element.elsevier-4efefa1e-9a8f-3ac1-a61f-9a723e9c9fa1

Marx, M. (2008). iSixSigma certification survey. *iSixSigma Magazine*, May/June.

Master Black Belt Certification MBB. (2019). ASQ. https://asq.org/cert/master-black-belt

Maslow, A. H. (1943). A theory of human motivation. *Psychological Review*, 50(4), 370.

McKeachie, W. J. (1978). *Teaching tips: A guidebook for the beginning college teacher* (7th ed.). Lexington, MA: D. C. Heath.

McKeon, K., Roccisano, J., Calisto, G., & Hill, W. J. (). "A helping hand- non-profit organization creates program to guide others through Six Sigma". *Six Sigma Forum Magazine*, August, 21–26.

McNair, P., & Mass, E. (2010). Applying design for six sigma to software and hardware systems. Safari Books Online, Sebastopol, CA. Retrieved from https://www.safaribooksonline.com/library/view/applying-design-for/ 9780137034093/?orpq

Mitra, A. (2004). Six sigma education: A critical role for academia. *The TQM Magazine*, 16(4), 293–302. doi:10.1108/09544780410541963

Noe, R. A. (2008). *Employee training and development*. New York, NY: McGraw-Hill.

Noe, R. A., & Colquitt, J. A. (2002). Planning for training impact: Principles of training effectiveness. In K. Kraiger (Ed.), *Creating, implementing, and managing effective training and development* (pp. 53–79). San Francisco, CA: Jossey-Bass.

Nogueira, D., Sousa, P., & Moreira, R. (2018). The relationship between leadership style and the success of Lean management implementation. *The Leadership & Organization Development Journal*, 39(6), 807–824.

Office for National Statistics (2016a). Definition of UK Service Industries. Retrived from http://webarchive.nationalarchives.gov.uk/ 20160109054646/http://www.ons.gov.uk/ons/rel/naa1-rd/national- accounts-articles/uk-service-industries–definition–classification-and- evolution/uk-service-industries-pdf.pdf. Accessed on August 16, 2019.

Office for National Statistics (2016b). Public Sector Personnel. Retrieved from https://www.ons.gov.uk/employmentandlabourmarket/peopleinwork/ publicsectorpersonnel. Accessed on August 16, 2019.

OECD (2015). Government at a Glance 2015. Retrived from http:// dx.doi.org/10.1787/gov_glance-2015-en. Accessed on August 21, 2019.

Pande, P., Neuman, R., & Cavanagh, R. (2000). *The Six Sigma way: How GE, Motorola and other top companies are honing their performance*. New York, NY: McGraw-Hill Professional.

Pappa, G. (2010, August 27). 3 challenges to overcome when developing a lean Six Sigma training curriculum. iSixSigma. Retrieved from https://www.isixsigma.com/training/3-challenges-overcome-when-developing-lean-six-sigma-training-curriculum/. Accessed on April 18, 2019.

Patel, S. (2017). How to overcome the biggest challenges in hiring top talent. *Inc.*, November 11. Retrieved from https://www.inc.com/sujan-patel/the-biggest-challenges-in-finding-top-talent-and-how-to-overcome-them.html. Accessed on April 17, 2019.

Peters, S. (2012). How GE is attracting, developing, and retaining global talent. *Harvard Business Review*, February 8.

Radic, K. (2013). Would you pass this Heineken job interview? *Brandingmag*, February 20. Retrieved from https://www.brandingmag.com/2013/02/20/heineken-the-candidate/. Accessed on April 17, 2019.

Random House. (1981). *Random House dictionary of the English language*. New York, NY: Random House.

Ready, D. A., Conger, J. A., & Hill, L. A. (2010). Are you a high potential? *Harvard Business Review*, 88, 78–84.

Rodgers, B., & Antony, J. (2019). Lean and Six Sigma practices in the public sector – A review. *International Journal of Quality & Reliability Management*, 36(3), 437–455.

Rodgers, B., Antony, J., Edgeman, R., & Cudney, E. (2019). Lean Six Sigma in the public sector: Yesterday, today, and tomorrow. *Total Quality Management & Business Excellence*, 1–13. doi:10.1080/14783363.2019.1599714

Ruben, B. R., Vinodh, S., & Asokan, P. (2017). Implementation of Lean Six Sigma framework with environmental considerations in an Indian automotive component manufacturing firm: A case study. *Production Planning & Control*, 28(15), 1193–1211.

Savolainen, T., & Haikonen, A. (2007). Dynamics of learning and continuous improvement in Six Sigma implementation. *The TQM Magazine*, 19(1), 6–17.

Schall, S. O. (2012). Variability reduction: A statistical engineering approach to engage operations teams in process improvement. *Quality Engineering*, 24(2), 264–279.

Schumacher, S. (2009). *High potential employees.* New York, NY: Prism Business Media.

Senge, P. (2006). *The fifth discipline – The art and practice of the learning organisation* (2nd ed.). New York, NY: Doubleday.

Setter, C. (2010). "Just say no to white belts", interview released to quality digest. Six Sigma Online. Retrieved from www.sixsigmaonline.org/six-sigma-training-certification-information/articles/just-say-noto-white-belts.html. Accessed on April 15, 2017.

SHL Talent Measurement. (2014). *"The HR Guide to Identifying High-Potentials."* CEB. https://www.ucop.edu/human-resources/management-development-program/2014/Donna%20Handout.pdf

Snee, R. D. (2009). Digging the holistic approach: Rethinking business improvement to improve the bottom-line. *Quality Progress*, October, pp. 52–54.

Snee, R. D., & Hoerl, R. W. (2003). *Leading Six Sigma – A step-by-step guide based on experience with GE and other Six Sigma companies.* Upper Saddle River, NJ: Financial Times/Prentice Hall.

Snee, R. D., & Hoerl, R. W. (2005). *Six Sigma beyond the factory floor; deployment strategies for financial services, health care, and the rest of the real economy.* Upper Saddle River, NJ: Financial Times/Prentice Hall.

Snee, R. D., & Hoerl, R. W. (2018). *Leading holistic improvement with Lean Six Sigma 2.0* (2nd ed.). North York: Pearson Education.

Snee, R. D., Kelleher, K. H., & Reynard, S. (1998). Improving team effectiveness. *Quality Progress*, May, pp. 43–48.

Sony, M., & Naik, S. (2012). Six Sigma, organisational learning and innovation. *International Journal of Quality & Reliability Management*, 29(8), 915–936.

Soto Gómez, E., Serván Núñez, M. J., Pérez Gómez, A. I., & Peña Trapero, N. (2015). Lesson study and the development of teacher's competences: From practical knowledge to practical thinking. *International Journal for Lesson and Learning Studies*, 4(3), 209–223. doi:10.1108/IJLLS-09-2014-0034.

Sunder, M. V. (2013). Six sigma: A strategy for increasing employee engagement. *Journal for Quality and Participation*, 36(2), 34–38.

Sunder, M. V. (2016). Lean Six Sigma in higher education institutions. *International Journal of Quality and Service Sciences*, 8(2), 159–178.

Sunder, M. V., & Antony, J. (2018). A conceptual Lean Six Sigma framework for quality excellence in higher education institutions. *International Journal of Quality & Reliability Management*, 35(4), 857–874.

Sunder, M. V., Ganesh, L. S., & Marathe, R. R. (2019). Lean Six Sigma in consumer banking–An empirical inquiry. *International Journal of Quality & Reliability Management*, 36(8), 1345–1369. doi:10.1108/IJQRM-01-2019-0012

Sunder, M. V., & Mahalingam, S. (2018). An empirical investigation of implementing Lean Six Sigma in higher education institutions. *International Journal of Quality & Reliability Management*, 35(10), 2157–2180.

Svinicki, M. D., & McKeachie, W. J. (2013). *McKeachie's teaching tips: Strategies, research, and theory for college and university teachers* (14th ed.). Belmont, CA: Cengage Learning.

Teece, D. J., Pisano, G., & Shuen, A. (1997). Dynamic capabilities and strategic management. *Strategic Management Journal*, 18(7), 509–533.

Tennant, C., & Roberts, P. (2001). Hoshin Kanri: Implementing the catchball process. *Long Range Planning*, 34(3), 287–308.

Tolman, A. (2001). In L. W. Anderson & D. R. Krathwohl, & B. S. Bloom (Eds.), *A taxonomy for learning, teaching, and assessing: A revision of Bloom's taxonomy of educational objectives*. New York, NY: Longman.

Van Assen, M. F. (2018). The moderating effect of management behavior for Lean and process improvement. *Operations Management Research*, 11(1–2), 1–13.

Waldman, D. A., Lituchy, T., Gopalakrishnan, M., Laframboise, K., Galperin, B., & Kaltsounakis, Z. (1998). A qualitative analysis of leadership and quality improvement. *The Leadership Quarterly*, 9(2), 177–201.

Weber, M. (1905). *The Protestant ethic and the spirit of capitalism: And other writings*. New York, NY: Penguin Group.

Welch, J. (2001). *Jack-straight from the gut.* New York, NY: Warner Business Books.

Wiggins, G., Wiggins, G. P., & McTighe, J. (2005). *Understanding by design.* Alexandria, VA: Association for Supervision and Curriculum Development.

Wilson, L. (2015). *How to implement lean manufacturing.* New York, NY: McGraw-Hill.

Wincel, J., & Kull, T. (2013). *People, process and culture.* London: Productivity Press.

Womack, J., & Jones, D. (2003). *Lean thinking: Banish waste and create wealth in your corporation.* London: Simon & Schuster.

Womack, J., Jones, D., & Roos, D. (2007). *The machine that changed the world.* London: Simon & Schuster, CPI Bath Press.

Womack, J. P., & Jones, D. T. (2005). Lean consumption. *Harvard Business Review, 83*(3), 58–68.

Yukl, G. A. (2006). *Leadership in organizations* (6th ed.). Prentice-Hall.

INDEX

Ability, 32, 80
Active participation, 10
Adaptation, 33
ADKAR, 79
Agile, 35–36, 38–41
Alignment, 9–16
American Express, 3
Analyse phase, 5
Aspiration, 32
Awareness, 80

Big Data, 110–112
Big Data Analytics (BDA), 110
Black Belts (BBs), 18, 23, 57–59
Bloom's taxonomy, 69
Businesses, 30
Business process improvement (BPI), 109

'Catchball' approach, 13
Career progression, 41–43
Carrots competition strategy, 78
Carrot stick strategy, 77–78
Carrot strategy, 76
Catalytic learning capability, 34
Cause and Effect Analysis, 5
Champions League, 29
Champion training, 58
Chart cumulative flow, 41
Commonwealth Health Corporation, 3
Communication, 48
Continuous improvement (CI), 1
Continuous learning, 34
Control Charts, 6
Control phase, 6
Cooperative learning, 62
Correlation Analysis, 5

Course preparation, 62
Critical success factors (CSFs), 30, 46
Critical-to-Quality drill-down tree, 5
Curriculum, 59–60
  assessment, 68–70
  development, 64–68
Customer satisfaction, 21

Define–Measure–Analyse– Improve–Control (DMAIC), 5, 24, 59, 93
Define phase, 5
360-Degree feedback mechanism, 40
Design for Lean Six Sigma (DFLSS), 91
Design of Experiments, 5
Desire, 80
Dow Chemical, 3
DuPont, 3
Dynamic capability, 91
Dynamic sensors, 34

Effort–impact matrix, 20
Employee satisfaction, 21
Engagement, 32
Enterprising spirit, 34
Environment Management System, 104
Establishing vision, 12
Executive talent, 31

Feedback, 61
Financial savings, 21
Formative assessment, 69
Ford, 3

Globalisation, 30
Green Belts (GBs), 18, 34, 57, 59
Green technology, 101–106

Heineken, 29
Higher educational systems, 116
High potential (HiPo) employees
   catalytic learning capability, 34
   critical top-level roles, 32
   drive to excel, 33
   dynamic sensors, 34
   enterprising spirit, 34
Histogram, 5
Honeywell, 2
Hoshin Kanri
   application, 9
   establishing vision, 12
   Lean Six Sigma (LSS), 13–15
   management, 11
   outcome, 9
   policy control, 13
   policy deployment, 12
   policy development, 12
   strategy deployment, 9
Hypothesis Testing, 5

Improve phase, 5
Innovation, 92–95
Insufficient time, 26
ISO 9001, 104
ISO 14001, 104

Knowledge, 48, 80, 96

Leaders, 33
Leadership, 6
   behaviours, 49–50
   characteristics, 50–51
   positions, 41–43
   skills, 47–49
   strategic significance, 47
   styles, 53–54
Lean, 1, 85
   high potentials, 34–35
   integration, 3–5
Lean Production System (LPS), 1, 2

Lean Six Sigma (LSS)
   Agile program, 36
   alignment, 9–16
   benefits, 4–5
   curriculum, 59–60
   emerging themes, 107–116
   green technology, 101–106
   HIPO selection process, 36–38
   innovation, 92–95
   leadership, 45–55
   methodology, 5–6
   organisational learning (OL), 96–99
   project selection and prioritisation, 17–27
   reward and recognition systems, 76–79
   sustainability, 83–89
   teaching and training, 60–61
   Ten Commandments, 1, 6–8
Lean Six Sigma strategy, 11
Learning, 97

3M, 3
Master Black Belts (MBBs), 57, 58
Measurement System Analysis (MSA), 5
Measure phase, 5
Monitoring and control, 27
Motivational theory, 74
Motorola, 2, 107

Non-value-added activities, 2

Organisational leaders, 85
Organisational learning (OL), 91, 96–99
Organisational strategy, 9–16

Pareto Chart, 5
Participants, 51
Phase-gate monitoring, 40
Poka-Yoke (Mistake-Proofing), 6
Policy control, 13
Policy deployment, 12
Policy development, 12
Prioritisation Matrix, 5

Index

Problem-solving, 23, 97
Process Capability Analysis, 5
Process Mapping, 5
Project Charter, 5
Project reviews, 23–25
Project selection
    criteria and score, 21, 22
    effort-impact matrix, 20
    failure, 25–27
    good and bad, 18–19
    responsible, 22–23
Public sector organisations, 114–115

Quality Management System, 104

Reinforcement, 80
Rewards and recognitions system, 73–75
    management strategy, 79–80
    types, 76–79
Risks, 21
Robotic Process Automation (RPA), 108–110
Root Cause Analysis, 5
Run Charts or Control Charts, 5

Scatter Diagram, 5
Self-determination theory, 74
Single Minute Exchange of Dies, 5
Six Sigma, 1
    high potentials, 34–35
    initiatives, 3
    integration, 3–5
    Motorola, 2
Small and medium enterprise (SME), 42
Soft skills training
    business process understanding, 63
    communication skills, 63
    leadership skills, 63
    management skills, 63–64
    positive attitude, 63
'Solution unknown' projects, 17
Spontaneous carrot strategy, 78–79
Sprints, 41

Standard Operating Procedures (SOP), 6
Statistical Engineering (SE), 113–114
Stick strategy, 77
Strategic alignment, 21
Summative assessment, 69–70
Supplier–Input–Process–Output–Customer (SIPOC), 5
Sustainability, 7, 70–71
    critical challenges, 84–87
    strategies to overcome, 87–89

Talent management, 30
Ten Commandments, 1, 6–8
Three Cs model, 53
Three Rs, 51
Time, 21
Top talent, 31–33
Total Quality Management (TQM), 92
Toyota, 46
Track velocity, 41
Training
    BBs, 58–59
    champion, 58
    GBs, 59
    MBBs, 58
    soft skills, 62–64
    YBs, 59
Transferring knowledge, 98
Transactional leadership, 54
Transformation, 49–50

Value-added activities, 2
Visual Management, 6
Voice of the Business (VOB), 23
Voice of the Customer (VOC), 5, 23

'War for Talent,' 31
WebProfits, 31

X-matrix, 13, 15

Yellow Belts (YBs), 34, 57, 59